PUBLIC SPEAKING

How to Rapidly Lose Fear & Excite Your Audience as a Confident Charismatic Speaker Without Anxiety

(Communicate With Ease and Survive in Any Situation)

David Carnegie

Published by Rob Miles

© **David Carnegie**

All Rights Reserved

Public Speaking: How to Rapidly Lose Fear & Excite Your Audience as a Confident Charismatic Speaker Without Anxiety (Communicate With Ease and Survive in Any Situation)

ISBN 978-1-989990-06-3

All rights reserved. No part of this guide may be reproduced in any form without permission in writing from the publisher except in the case of brief quotations embodied in critical articles or reviews.

Legal & Disclaimer

The information contained in this book is not designed to replace or take the place of any form of medicine or professional medical advice. The information in this book has been provided for educational and entertainment purposes only.

The information contained in this book has been compiled from sources deemed reliable, and it is accurate to the best of the Author's knowledge; however, the Author cannot guarantee its accuracy and validity and cannot be held liable for any errors or omissions. Changes are periodically made to this book. You must consult your doctor or get professional medical advice before using any of the suggested remedies, techniques, or information in this book.

Upon using the information contained in this book, you agree to hold harmless the Author from and against any damages, costs, and expenses, including any legal fees potentially resulting from the application of any of the information provided by this guide. This disclaimer applies to any damages or injury caused by the use and application, whether directly or indirectly, of any advice or information presented, whether for breach of contract, tort, negligence, personal injury, criminal intent, or under any other cause of action.

You agree to accept all risks of using the information presented inside this book. You need to consult a professional medical practitioner in order to ensure you are both able and healthy enough to participate in this program.

Table of Contents

INTRODUCTION 1

CHAPTER 1: PUTTING SUCCESS IN THE WORKS 4

CHAPTER 2: BEFORE THE PRESENTATION 11

CHAPTER 3: HOW YOUR NERVOUS SYSTEM'S FEAR RESPONSE WORKS 30

CHAPTER 4: ON THE EDGE 34

CHAPTER 5: ARISTOTLE'S THREE MEANS OF PERSUASION AND CICERO'S FIVE CANONS OF RHETORIC 47

CHAPTER 6: ARE YOU A BORN SPEAKER? 58

CHAPTER 7: VISUALISE A BETTER YOU 62

CHAPTER 8: WAYS PUBLIC SPEAKING CAN IMPROVE YOUR LIFE 75

CHAPTER 9: THE POWER OF YOUR WORDS 82

CHAPTER 10: DEALING WITH MANAGEABLE SPEAKING ANXIETIES 94

CHAPTER 11: SHOULD I VIDEOTAPE MYSELF GIVING A SPEECH AS PRACTICE? 109

CHAPTER 12: HOW TO USE APPROPRIATE TECHNIQUES WHEN ADDRESSING AN AUDIENCE DIRECTLY OR USING A MICROPHONE/ LOUDSPEAKER SYSTEM. 117

CHAPTER 13: THE STRUCTURE AND OUTLINE OF A GREAT SPEECH 122

CHAPTER 14: TIPS AND STRATEGIES TO MAKE PRESENTATIONS WITH CONFIDENCE 126

CHAPTER 15: TALK! DON'T READ 132

CHAPTER 16: LEARN TO COERCE NICELY--USE YOUR CHARM! 135

CHAPTER 17: WHAT TO AVOID WHEN SPEAKING IN PUBLIC. 141

CHAPTER 18: YOU ARE NOT ALONE 153

CHAPTER 19: STORIES AND ANECDOTES 158

CHAPTER 20: BRIEF INTRODUCTION 167

CHAPTER 21: QUALITATIVE DESCRIPTIONS ACTIVITY 171

CHAPTER 22: SIZE MATTERS 176

CONCLUSION 183

Introduction

Public speaking is one of the most influential skills you can learn. It allows you to share your thoughts and ideas with the world. It can motivate others to take action, inspire individuals to see beyond their current circumstances and it can entertain and make others laugh. There is one thing that all leaders throughout history have in common: they are all excellent public speakers. Today we live in a world where technology and social media drive much of the way in which we communicate, yet the power of public speaking has not diminished. Many major announcements in the world are still shared through a speech or a presentation. Just think of Apple, Microsoft, TED and off course political announcements.

In this book we share with you how to master the art of public speaking by considering three key stages:

The first stage is the **character development stage**. The public speaking journey does not begin the moment you stand on stage to deliver a speech. Nor does it begin when you start writing and practicing a speech. It begins when you make a decision to start working on your inner self. In this stage we consider how to develop the mindset of a public speaker, how to overcome the fear of public speaking and how to speak from the heart.

The second stage is the **speech preparation stage**. There is a common misconception about public speaking - many people think that speeches require little preparation. The truth is, public speaking requires significant preparation and practice. No-one is born a natural speaker. In this stage we share tips on how to write a speech, how to make a speech easy to understand and how to practice your speech.

The third stage is the **speech delivery stage**. This is often what many people think of when they want to learn public speaking. However, success in this stage relies upon a strong foundation - a well developed character together with a well prepared speech. In this stage we share how to have a captivating voice, how to have an engaging eye contact and how to use body language effectively.

Visualise the three stages as an iceberg. We only get to see it's tip but there is a huge mass that lies beneath the surface. In public speaking, the audience only gets to see the third stage: delivery, but the hard work occurs behind the scenes during the character development and the speech preparation stages.

Chapter 1: Putting Success In The Works

A lot of people fail to deliver effective public speaking for several reasons. One of which is the lack of preparation. To be able to come up with great public speaking is to take into account many prerequisites. The first thing to understand about public speaking is that it is the product of skills and preparation combined.

Public speaking is not something that you just do without first being prepared. If you do that, the result on your part would be chaotic. You'd need to leverage your strengths making it possible to overcome the weak points in your delivery. To be prepared, you must ask yourself a couple of questions like:

What are my strengths?

What are my weaknesses?

Do I have all the skills I need?

Explore yourself. Assess the things you have and the things you don't. It would help if you had someone to guide you through this process. Like they always say, "two heads are better than one." First off you need to understand your strengths. Now, these can be anything that you're good at that would help you deliver a better presentation. Having a clear, crisp voice for instance, is one good quality that you could have. If not, you might need to look into that because a great public speaking requires your voice to be heard, not just by the few people fronting you but by everyone across the room. Also, you must consider looking into the things that you don't have. Think of the things that you're not good at. Be honest when you think about this because it's going to help you out a lot. Don't think of it as a bad thing to find yourself lacking but rather think of it as room for improvement. Having a good perspective is a really useful tool in improving yourself.

First up, take a recorder, do a sample presentation and listen to your voice carefully. Try to listen to the recording a couple of times and look for any irregularities or things that you think you should not do. Most often, our tone of voice, choice of words, and the delivery of our sentences mean a lot or it could have a huge impact on the outcome of your presentation.

Saying Things Correctly

When you are going to do a presentation, it help to do some research on your topic. Invest your time on finding the right pronunciation of words and jargon. What you say is totally important. However, the way you say it is equally as important. In a nutshell, diction is a very important factor in a great public speaking. The words you say and how you say them is extremely necessary. Slurring your words or won't do you any good.

When pressed with time and you're just halfway through, you might need to speed up a little bit. Speaking too slow would take up too much time. Speaking too fast, however, will only make it faster for your audience to lose interest and probably be annoyed by your delivery. It's all about pacing, dictation, and clarity. It's when the audience fully grasps and understand each word you say that you can conclude you had a great public speaking experience.

If you're not quite sure on where to start, better begin with the basics. Do some diction exercises to get your tongue in shape. Just like athletes do warm ups before they start a game, or the way singers vocalize before each performance, a good public speaker must also be prepared to speak, and utter words with clarity. If it helps, you could try out some tongue twisters preferably from A-Z. This will get your tongue get used to different words plus enabling your brain to memorize each and every one of them. The main purpose of doing articulation exercises is to set up a pattern of better, more enhanced way of speaking. Plus, it also allows the muscle groups involved in speech to be stretched and strengthened. Although it may sound unnecessary but there will always come a time where you encounter words that are just hard to pronounce especially when trying to pronounce words from a foreign language. Having and honing the ability to speak clearly is essential in public speaking as it mainly involves speech. Other than learning to articulate each word you say, you also need to learn some other public speaking preparations.

Abiding the 3 C's of Public Speaking

Public speaking is all about conveying a message to your audience and how well you do it. To be able to give a great presentation you must be able to follow the four C's of public speaking:

Content – what will your message be? Be sure not to forget to ask yourself this question. Before anything else, take some time to conceptualize your content. Think about the stuff that you need to discuss and the things that you should not. Although you may have a lot in mind and want to say them all, you might not get that chance to tell everything because it might not be appropriate or it might deviate to a whole new topic. Conceptualize, create, and plan your execution. It's always necessary to map out all the areas you're going to discuss and those you don't

Confidence – gearing up for public speaking demands a huge amount of confidence. Standing in front of a huge crowd alone requires great confidence. Practice is always the best tool to gain confidence. When you master your content, do a mockup presentation and have someone rate it for you. This will give you the idea of whether or not you're going to fail or succeed. Adding confidence to yourself is a matter of faith. Belief that will enable you to do what it is that you need to do. It will also allow you to expand your boundaries daring yourself to go beyond what you're used to and embracing the fact that you could always do more. With that in mind, it's easy to feel confident anytime you want.

Contribution – public speaking is all about conveying a message. However, you must also consider the value of your message and how it can contribute to the betterment of your listeners. It must not only be you who will benefit from your presentation but also for those who have listened. It's just like having a conversation. It can be something that you would forget the next minute or a really good thing that you will carry within you for a very long time.

Chapter 2: Before The Presentation

(setting yourself up for success...or for horrible, horrible failure)

Now it will be helpful to go into a little depth regarding things you **should** do, good practices to get into, and steps you can take to make your presentation more successful. There is a quote that drives to the heart of much of what this chapter will try to convey, from former Arizona State Senator and professional speaker Somers White:

"90% of how well the talk will go is determined before the speaker steps on the platform."

The good news about this is that, no matter how you feel about your own abilities to talk in front of a crowd, a large part of your success will have little to do with the actual talking-in-front-of-a-crowd part. Of course, this also means you have a good amount of preparation in front of you before even getting up on the platform to speak.

Know Your Subject Matter

I think it probably goes without saying that you should Know Your Subject Matter. When I first started teaching at Sub School, I had just left my submarine as the most senior Junior Officer (the grouping of lieutenants and junior on the boat who are on their first sea tour). When you've spent 32+ months assigned to the sub and have been fully qualified to oversee operations of the entire vessel from the nuclear engine room back aft all the way up forward through the sonar dome at the nosecone, you (usually) have a pretty good level of expertise at what it takes to operate the sub in port and at sea. Even so, I had a fair number of late nights preparing for my first class of teaching the Submarine School curriculum to brand new ensigns, many of whose only submarine experience was during summer training as college students for no longer than a couple weeks at most. I think most people recognize that there are differences in what you learn formally in a classroom or seminar, and how that information is actually utilized in practice in the real world. If you spend too long in one realm or the other, you might need to refresh yourself on the other side of things.

Also, realize that there is a decent chance you will have somebody ask you a clarifying question during your presentation, or ask you to expound upon something you mentioned. Depending on the situation of your presentation (are you a subject matter expert teaching a group who expects you to be thoroughly trained in a topic, or were you "volun-told" that you'd be spending 15 minutes talking about a mandatory subject that nobody really cares about?), the chances of this may vary. Either way, it doesn't hurt to go through what you'll be talking about and try to think about any peripherally-related topics or in-depth thoughts that a student might have on the subject. You don't want to have the deer-in-the-headlights look as you stammer your way through a response because you've been caught off guard by someone in your audience.

Know Your Audience

Besides knowing your subject matter, you should do your best to Know Your Audience. Most of the time you're going to be getting up to teach, you'll probably have an idea of who is out in the crowd. That information can help guide how you give your presentation, the time you spend on various topics, the subject matter overall, the way you interact with the audience members, and so on. If I'm teaching an official course to certify people in CPR, I might be teaching it to a group of school teachers, babysitters, and lifeguards who have never taken it before, a handful of nurses who work in the healthcare field at a rural general practitioner's office and only know the topic in theory, or veteran paramedics and firefighters doing yet another refresher course and who have worked cardiac arrest patients more times than they can recall. For each of these groups, I might talk about the same general information and deliver more or less the same message, but I'm going to do it in significantly different ways, focusing on different specific items, and presenting myself in somewhat of a different manner for each.

Similarly, I'm going to have slightly different ways of presenting information (whether in regards to formality, depth of topic, or in other manners) to small groups vs. large groups, experienced officers vs. new junior officers, or business peers vs. senior company leadership. Overall my personality and a lot of the characteristics in which I give presentations don't change – nobody has ever accused me of **too** much formality during a presentation – but how I interact with the audience relating to the topic at hand will.

It benefits you to make sure you have an idea of who will be in your audience, how big the audience is, and their level of experience. It's helpful to know this because that will help you figure out what they want to hear and how they want to hear it. If you don't tailor your discussion to your audience, they're not going to be particularly interested in what you have to say.

If you don't know your audience ahead of time, then you'll just have to do your best to give the presentation as you've been asked to, and read the audience as your presentation goes on in order to modify your tone or content as necessary on the fly.

Know Your Presentation

Another thing you need to do ahead of time is Know Your Presentation. This is different that knowing your subject matter. Just because you have an overall good grasp of your subject matter does not mean you don't need to look through the lecture you're going to give beforehand and be familiar with how it will be presented. In one course I took, the lecturer had a degree specific to the topic at hand and had been through the same training course himself at one point. Even so, he would click and transition to a slide, see some concept mentioned in a bullet point, and then wonder out loud if the slideshow went into that particular topic in more depth later in the presentation. Things like that — clear indications that you're unfamiliar with the presentation you're giving — undermine the credibility and expertise you might otherwise have. Something like that is a relatively minor problem if you're otherwise competent as a presenter and subject matter expert. However, if you struggle as an instructor **and** it's clear you haven't even looked through the slide show before giving it, then your students are not likely to have too favorable an opinion of your capabilities.

Back to my preparing into the evenings during shore duty prior to teaching my first Sub School classes — just because I spent years stationed on a submarine doesn't mean that I know the layout of every school class module on the topic before teaching it, the intent of every slide in every lecture, or detailed knowledge of every shipboard system or component that a lecture mentions. There were many times where I had experience with a slightly different piece of equipment or system software build than what the slideshow discussed. And occasionally, there are simply things that you **should** know about your topic, but that for whatever reason managed to get past you when you were first learning and you never ran into a situation where you needed to know them. It's much better to realize that the day before your presentation when you have time to panic slightly and seek out the answer from anybody who might have it, than to not know the topic will come up at all in your discussion until you click on the slide and see your first bullet point is something you were completely unprepared to talk about. By the time your ignorance has made itself known to everybody sitting down and staring at you while you stumble through a mealy-mouthed explanation of why that particular thing isn't important and you're not going to talk about it, it's too late to wish you would have spent an extra half hour the night before making sure that nothing is going to surprise you in the slideshow you're giving.

Those points are all important to keep in mind if you'll be giving a presentation that you didn't create. However, there are a few things to perhaps help when developing your own slideshow.

First, your slideshow doesn't **have** to be some super-polished, amazing presentation worthy of admiration from world-class consulting firms. I've seen people show presentations that were black text bullet points on plain white background slides. They also happened to give engaging, interesting lectures. In those cases, the slideshow was a very limited supporting character in the show and the presenter could have done just as well alone up in front of the audience without a screen to refer to. That **is** an option. That option also has the added inherent benefit of not violating several of the "Don'ts" from up above.

However, most people will probably want to add some level of personalization to their slideshows. For me, I tend to pepper unnecessarily ridiculous items throughout the lecture. I was giving a presentation during a sales summit attended by about 20 people including the top company executives. In one slide in the middle of the presentation, a small photo of the vice president's head slowly popped in and out from the bottom of the slide on a several-second delay. I had a large headshot photo of the Chief Operations Officer turn in circles with the Batman TV show transition music playing a couple times spontaneously when moving between topics throughout the slideshow. I'll make completely non-sequitur animations of a photo of some object doing some random action for no reason (which will inevitably take longer on its own to put together than the rest of the presentation combined). The key for me is: I know what I think is stupid but funny, and also have an idea of what the crowd I'm talking to will think is at least mildly entertaining in the middle of a slideshow. And in the midst of an otherwise professional, smooth-flowing talk, I'll do one of these unexpected things and get people refocused a little bit.

That happens to work for me and my personality; it might not work for yours. Don't force a presentation that obviously doesn't work for you. Also, don't just find some PowerPoint on the internet that relates to the topic you're going to talk about and use that without making any changes to personalize it a little bit. Make it a presentation that's representative of you and your organization.

Know Your Talking Points

Somewhat related to knowing your presentation, but that requires an additional level of preparation, is to Know Your Talking Points. This is where the bulk of the preparation really takes place, and there are multiple things that tie into it. I've heard from a few places that somebody should spend about two to four hours preparing for every one hour that the actual presentation is supposed to last. In my experience, that's about accurate. It's **especially** accurate for presentations that you create yourself and that aren't part of a pre-existing curriculum or training program. Any time that I've created my own lecture for something, it has taken at least several hours to put my thoughts down, cull extra information from the internet or other sources that is relevant to include, put together handouts if applicable, lay everything out in a slideshow, search for any applicable multimedia that can help make a point and keep things interesting, fine-tune any effects that I want the slideshow to have, and then practice and refine the presentation itself.

The last thing I mentioned there was to "practice the presentation itself." Yes – you should rehearse your presentation. Unlike while teaching a formal course full time, where I could go to any number of empty classrooms where I worked, stand up front, and give a full-fledged presentation in the same environment in which I would be teaching it to actual students, that's not often as available in many business situations. Still, if I'm preparing any type of presentation, I will close my office door, put the presentation on my computer, physically stand up, and go through the slideshow as though I'm delivering it to somebody. I'll use the voice inflections and physical gestures that I'd make with an actual audience (albeit at a slightly lower speaking level...). I'll time myself and see how long it takes, adding or cutting as necessary. I'll find any stumbling blocks in my bullet points. I'll figure out any transitions that I didn't realize were awkward when I was just moving slides around in PowerPoint. I'll think of a story or example to use that didn't come to me earlier when I was just sitting at a desk quietly typing out the thoughts. I'll figure out if the notes I wrote down in my instructor guide (which I'll discuss shortly) are too hard to decipher when I'm actually standing and moving around. There are all sorts of benefits to actually standing up and rehearsing what you'll be demonstrating to the group, especially if it's a talk you've never given before or if you're not used to getting in front of an audience. It could be argued that, if avoiding all those "Don't" items from the beginning is the quickest way to help your presentation be Not Bad, rehearsing your talk ahead of time might be the best way to move your presentation toward actually being Good. There are so many little mistakes you catch and improvements you can make from rehearsing just once, that it adds up to a lot of benefit in the end.

Like I alluded to above, one thing that you should also do whenever you're giving a presentation is to print out the slides and prepare an Instructor Guide. Every lecture would be printed out, four or six slides per page, and would have notes handwritten on them to help keep things on track. Once you're standing in front of an audience, you won't remember every question you meant to ask the students at a certain point in the slides, or every preparatory transition you were going to make before clicking on a particular slide coming up, or every (hopefully amusing) little anecdote you were going to tell to help reinforce one of your points at a specific time. Jotting down those notes on your own guide will help you remember them and give you a smoother flow when you're actually giving the presentation. If I don't occasionally glance at my instructor guide, it's guaranteed I'll get wrapped up in doing the presentation and completely miss making some particularly cogent or moderately entertaining point that I really wanted to talk about.

Know Your Backup Plan

The concept of having an instructor guide will segue right into Know Your Backup Plan. Another hypothetical question: Have you ever been at a presentation where the technology threatened not to work (computer wouldn't connect to the projector, presentation wouldn't come up, sound wouldn't work, etc.) or ended up actually not working altogether? Yeah...that sucks. It's especially bad for somebody who put a lot of work into making a compelling slideshow or had engaging multimedia to include with their discussion. So yes, it really is too bad to spend hours preparing something that no one will ever see. But now it's time to put on your big-boy/big-girl pants, accept the reality that your slideshow is gone, and be the one responsible for making it or breaking it from here. You have to have a backup plan.

Part of that backup plan is printing out the slides on paper that you'll be using and be prepared to talk about them...in front of the audience...without the slideshow behind you (gasp!). Fortunately, you already printed out your instructor guide, so not only do you have the main content of your talk in front of you, but you also have all the stories, examples, questions, notes, and smooth transitions that you had planned out ahead of time to help you get through things. The downside is that obviously you don't have a good visual representation of the lesson you're trying to teach to everybody, and it's often more awkward feeling to stand up in front of a crowd with just **you** to lead the discussion than to have a slideshow behind you to help draw the attention toward. On the plus side – everybody is now giving you a lot more leeway to do the job. Most people are sympathetic when things don't work out as planned and they're just glad it's happening to you and not them. If you have a sensible, coherent, modestly informative presentation to make based off the notes you're holding, and you were able to do it **despite** technology slapping you in the face in front of everybody, you win.

Having your printed-out notes ready to go is one way to help with your backup plan. That's not the only thing you should do, though. If I'm giving a presentation, I usually keep it on my laptop, and bring my own computer to wherever it is I'm going to be talking. I bring my own power cord and audio/visual cables to connect to a projector just in case the facility I'm going do doesn't have them for some reason.

You should also have a backup of your actual presentation. While I have the copy I created on my own laptop, I'll also save a copy to a thumb drive in case I need to use somebody else's computer, and I'll email myself a copy in case the thumb drive doesn't work for some reason and I still have an internet connection. It doesn't take too long to do any of these steps, but it gives you a variety of options for the unknown situation that is desperately trying to undermine your presentation in any way possible.

Overall, the difficulty level of performing a scheduled training or presentation when something goes wrong may very well be caused and exacerbated by technology failures, but the inability to do it altogether generally lies with the instructor themselves.

Chapter 3: How Your Nervous System's Fear Response Works

Watch the video

Fear works according to certain rules that are hard-wired in your brain and nervous system.

It all starts with the emotional part of your brain. Your emotional brain is more primitive and instinctual than your thinking brain, which evolved centuries later. Your thinking brain is responsible for higher executive functions like language and reasoning. And as we'll see in this course, mastering public speaking fear requires understanding how your emotional brain and thinking brain work together.

Your emotional brain acts as your personal security guard - on the lookout for any possible danger. It's crucial for surviving dangers, and it's hard-wired to immediately trigger a whole series of emergency responses without even thinking.

For example, if you're hiking, your emotional brain will be the first to detect a rattlesnake coiled in your path and will cause your body to react reflexively and instantly to protect yourself. Your emotional brain will get your body ready in a split second to either run from the snake or fight the snake without even thinking about it. The instantaneous fear response is a reflex - like blinking your eye and it's meant to protect you from physical danger.

When your emotional brain detects something that might be dangerous, it sends a message to your sympathetic nervous system to release a chemical cocktail into your body. These chemicals then give you a burst of energy so you can run from the danger or fight the danger. One of the chemicals is adrenaline, which causes rapid heart rate, rapid breathing, sweating, and other natural fear symptoms.

The fear response is a normal reaction that everyone experiences in response to a perceived threat. But notice that we used the word perceived. It doesn't have to be a real threat. Even when you imagine frightening things that could happen, your emotional brain interprets that as a real threat, and it triggers the fear response. So your thoughts, ideas and imagination can trigger the fear response. Let's see how this works with public speaking. When your emotional brain thinks you might receive a negative evaluation or that there's a threat to important relationships, it sends an alert to your sympathetic nervous system to release adrenaline and other chemicals. This causes the typical public speaking symptoms such as sweaty palms, faster heart rate, difficulty breathing and so on. Your brain uses this primitive security system whether it's a physical threat or a social threat. The burst of adrenaline is intended to protect us from physical dangers but it's confusing when these biological emergency responses go off in social situations. The good news is that once you understand what's happening, you can take action.

Chapter 4: On The Edge

"If you do it, I'll do it!"

That's what three of my friends said in Queenstown, New Zealand after my mum had offered to pay for me to bungee jump, knowing full well that I was afraid of heights. A list of pros and cons screamed in my head, convincing me first to do it, then not to, then to do it again, until I finally came to a decision; I was going to do it. There's nothing like a 20-year old's ego and three of his best mates applying friendly peer pressure to get you to jump off a perfectly good bridge with a raging river 50m below it.

"Look up, pretend you are brave; and whatever you, do make sure your jump is good."

Those were the encouraging words of the instructor, after she found out we might buy the DVD recording.

"Do you want to get wet?"

"I guess so…" I responded hesitantly, not really sure if I did want to get wet.

"Good; because you are over 100kg, so you don't have an option."

Great. I was going to get wet whether I liked it or not. Had I really had an option at any stage in the process so far?

I was first up. I felt like Eminem in 8 Mile; "palms are sweaty, knees weak, arms are heavy", though thankfully, so far, no vomit on my sweater, but it felt like it wasn't far off. The feeling of intense nerves was overpowering.

You see I'm generally a pretty calm collected guy. I try and live life by a mantra my rugby coach gave to us:

"Ain't no use worrying about things beyond your control, because if they're beyond your control, ain't no use worrying. Ain't no use worrying about things within your control, because if you have them under control, ain't no use worrying."

– Mickey Rivers

Sitting on the ledge watching the person before me get the opposite of a hostage 'jumper' talk down to get them to jump, I felt like it was impossible to live to this mantra.

I ran a checklist in my head.

Things in my control: Jumping off the bridge to then make everything outside of my control.

Things out of my control: Everything else.

This is when my amygdala, the area in your brain responsible for fear, kicked into overdrive and everything else in there switched off. My breathing became rapid, I could feel my heart trying to beat out of my chest, a cold sweat had taken over my body and I had the shakes. This was not something I had felt in a very long time.

My brain took me back to the last time I had this sense of helplessness. Back to my first year at high school before stepping on stage for my first ever speech.

Was this the end for me? Was my life flashing before my eyes before I had even jumped? Look up, look brave, jump high. I just kept repeating this over and over to myself as I watched the teared-up lady before me finally jump.

"You're up, mate. Just hold on to this bar and shuffle towards the end of the platform." I grabbed the bar and began to shuffle forward. Look up, look brave, jump high.

"Ok mate, now let go of the bar and shuffle right to the edge."

What? There was no mention of this ten seconds ago. That pole was the difference between me standing and looking, and me being exposed to falling off the ledge. It was one of the only things I had in my control that was making me feel some semblance of separation from the impending plummet into the river below. Slowly I loosened my grip off the pole, one finger at a time.

What felt like a big gust of wind hit me. I wanted to reach back to the pole behind me, but that would involve blindly reaching and throwing out my balance.

"Five…Four…Three…" Where did this countdown come from? It got me even more flustered.

"Two…One." Look up, look brave, jump high.

I've jumped. I'm hurtling down towards the river below. Free falling for what feels like an eternity, but like a split second at the same time. Pshhh! I hit the water and recoiled back up 30 metres into the air. It feels like my body is all out of balance, so I am flailing around like a salmon in a bear's mouth. Everything now is completely outside of my control.

After the jump when we compared the emotional rollercoaster we all went on, I found it interesting how similar the experience was.

We all achieved the same result of completing a bungee jump, but the actual jump itself was so different.

My jump was fairly stock standard; my friend Simon sprung in the air like a frog and dived straight down like an Olympic diver; and Marc ripped his shirt off and leaped backwards. Rory, however, bent his knees all set for a huge jump, but at the bottom of his knees bending, had second thoughts and tried to reach back to grab the pole. His centre of gravity took him over the edge in a crouched over, twisted tangle.

It fascinates me to think about all the similarities between bungy jumping and when I first spoke on stage.

It was a Maori speech competition I had been somewhat forcefully entered in as one of the few eligible from my school, as I had New Zealand Maori Heritage.

Being thirteen at the time, it's fair to assume it was most of the speakers' first time in front of an audience; particularly one with a few hundred people in it.

So, with all of us feeling similar levels of fear and anxiety before our talks, why was it that some of the talks looked like the equivalent of the slick backward bungee jump, some like my run of the mill jump and others showed their fear like they were trying to reach back for the safety pole mid-jump?

The answers most of you think is that they are more confident, have the gift of the gab or were better prepared.

This book is going to dispel all those myths.

I, for one, was a confident kid struck down with fear and had to read off cue cards. I have met and trained hundreds of confident adults who were horrible at presenting in front of groups and effectively sharing a message; not to mention the others who avoided speaking altogether.

You see, my speech in that contest was very similar to my bungee jump. Nothing flash, far from memorable for anyone watching, and lots of correction along the way trying to get back on course.

Rather than Look up, look brave, jump high, it was more along the lines of Look up (between cue cards), look brave (stand up tall), jump high (read loudly)". I put read loudly there because with cue cards in my hands that is literally what I was doing.

Unsurprisingly I didn't win that day. Thankfully though, I am rather competitive. This competitive streak and youthful ignorance led me to ask myself a question; how can I improve?

The last 18+ years has been spent continually looking to refine the answer. To work towards not only mastery for myself, but simplicity to be able to teach this and transform others.

We have all heard it; people would rather be dead than speak in public. 78% of people suffer from speech anxiety, which must mean 4/5 people reading this would rather be in the casket than give the eulogy.

Look I get it, I truly do.

Even when I had started to learn the craft of public speaking, I had that fear. I'm not even joking!

When I was 14, my mum made me give a eulogy on behalf of our family at my great aunt's funeral. I went through a raft of emotions; fear, embarrassment, sadness, and the real worry that I wouldn't do the eulogy justice for someone important to me. Throw in the fact that this was this was the first funeral I had ever been to, and there was only two of us speaking; myself and a cousin.

Here's the thing though; this wasn't just any cousin. He was a highly accomplished speaker whom had been knighted by the Queen. Thankfully, a funeral isn't a competition, but it's always nice if the bar isn't set too high to follow up with.

He went up first and gave an amazing speech... in two languages!

It's fair to say that did not help calm my nerves or center my raft of emotions.

The thing was at that stage where there was a lot I didn't understand. Important things, like the physiology of what occurs in the brain to cause the fear I was experiencing.

I hadn't identified a system to not only mitigate fear, but produce a high-quality talk every time (Yes, even a eulogy).

I held back sobbing and managed to share a message from the heart that I know was appreciated by our family.

Afterwards, just like the time a year ago on stage at that speech competition, I knew that I could do better. That there must be an easier, more effective and less nerve-wracking way.

With any skill you are looking to improve, it's more about finding out what you don't know as much as it is knowing what you don't know. It was around this time I doubled down on my endeavour to become the speaker I knew I could.

Tony Robbins often says "the fastest way to get from where you are to where you want to be is to find someone who is there and model them.".

When the student is ready, the teacher will appear. Thankfully for me, that teacher, Mrs Donna Jones, appeared and helped change my thoughts and approach towards speaking. She helped instil a system and confidence that has been responsible for countless opportunities I have created and taken.

If you have picked up this book, hopefully you are ready for a change. Let me be your teacher.

My goal for this book is to help two types of people. For those who have never really given any type of public speaking a go, I'm going to give you a foolproof system to fast track you into being a confident powerful speaker; and for the more experienced speakers, you'll get the strategic ways to control and influence a talk to give more value and achieve your speaking goals.

We're going to cover three main secrets for becoming a confident public speaker.

Secret 1: Fear Elimination; How to quickly and easily identify and eliminate all the fear that has been holding you back from public speaking.

Secret 2: Talk Creation; How to implement my proven public speaking blueprint and implement my 30% rule so that every speech no matter the situation or preparation time is amazing.

Secret 3: Exposure; How to create opportunities in your business, brand or job with these 3 free techniques.

This is exactly what I have done over time to build and leverage my credibility in different industries, get in front of more of my ideal prospects and positively impact more people.

I'm on a mission to make speaking more enjoyable to give, and more importantly more enjoyable to listen to and for you to be able to share your message with a wider audience.

What follows in the book will give you the tools and frameworks to do all of that and more.

Chapter 5: Aristotle's Three Means Of Persuasion And Cicero's Five Canons Of Rhetoric

In this chapter, you will be equipped with the practical knowledge on Aristotle's Three Means of Persuasion and Cicero's Five Canons of Rhetoric. If you intend to take these topics in the university, it might take you a semester or two to cover these topics.

In this compendium, efforts were taken to simplify these concepts so that you can apply it in your preparation and delivery of public speeches. Note that if you are serious with acquiring the essentials of rhetoric, you should concentrate on mastering these concepts which are handed down to us from the Classic Period.

Aristotle's Three Means of Persuasion

According to the great Greek Scholar Aristotle, you need to master the art of persuasion if you wish to become an effective public speaker. There are many ways to persuade an audience, but according to him, each instance will fall down ultimately into three classifications. The first means pertain to the character and morals of the speaker. The second mode concentrates on the art of preparing the audience's heart so that they will be ready for the framework of thinking that you want them to acquire. The third and last method gives emphasis on the manner of proving the speaker's points.

Means of Persuasion #1: The Ethos

The ethos refers to the speaker's appeal to reputation or character. If you want to persuade thousands of people to believe what you have to say, your character and reputation should pave the way for your authority. There are many people who are capable of crafting rather impressive thoughts that are backed up by logical empirical proof. However, if the person who says it does not have the credibility, the audience would most likely choose not to believe him.

According to Aristotle, the ethos of the speaker is composed of several layers. The credibility of the speaker is first assessed by virtue of his personal knowledge and expertise in relation to the topic at hand. The other factor being assessed by the audience is the speaker's character and morals. Therefore, in any speech, according to both Aristotle and Cicero, the speaker should spend the first few moments building his credibility in order to make him a believable resource person on the subject at hand.

However, another rhetorician by the name of Isocrates believed that a man should make sure that he is a man of character even before he delivers his speech. Therefore, if you want to influence other people via public speaking, you should do everything within your power to maintain a clean record so that you will be considered as a reliable and trustworthy source of information.

There are many ways to build on your ethos. First, you may start your speech by mentioning that you are an expert on the topic. You can say the length of time you have spent studying the particular subject. If applicable, you can mention parallel efforts that you have made in order to be an expert in that field. Likewise, mentioning your awards and recognitions might help.

Another way to do it is by living a virtuous life. This may be the foolproof way of developing your ethos. Most people find it easy to detect any trace of hypocrisy, so you have to be very careful with the manner you deliver your speech. But if you are confident that you are leading an honest, earnest, and virtuous life, then there is nothing to worry about.

Means of Persuasion #2: The Pathos

The pathos refers to the method by which a speaker touches the emotion of the audience. Aristotle does not dismiss the fact that this is a very effective route to persuasion. While many put specific focus on crafting logical arguments, history has proven that this particular mode of persuasion should never be neglected by any aspiring public speaker.

When logic combats logic, the runaway winner is the stronger argument. However, if the battle is between reason and emotion, usually, emotion wins. Don't frown upon this fact because it's human nature that is being described here. Take for example the advertisements that dominate the airwaves. Truth be told, they are able to market their products and sell their services because they do well with appealing to people's emotions.

How do you apply this to your speeches in the future then? You can start with integrating emotion to your arguments. That's not very difficult to do, actually. All you have to know your audience and think of arguments that they can relate to. If they can relate to what you are saying, there is a better chance that you will capture their hearts. Also, you can input some storytelling and metaphors into your speech.

These will also help in adding color to your piece. If you will have a visual presentation, you can pick images that can stir your audience's emotion. For example, if you are talking about poverty, you can show children who are working at a young age or babies who suffer from hunger. For sure, such images, along with your explanation will break your listeners' hearts.

Means of Persuasion #3: The Logos

The final means of persuasion, as discussed by Aristotle, is the logos or the appeal to reason. Aristotle personally believed that logos is the most superior among the means of persuasion. After all, it is difficult to defend a faulty argument; hence, it is the responsibility of every public speaker to strengthen his reasoning skills. Though no debate is won by reason alone, one should not neglect the power of the intellect. There may be times when even the audience may not be that sophisticated to understand many of your arguments, but a sound argument is like a well-established wall that a public speaker can rely on any time of the day.

In Aristotle's **The Art of Rhetoric,** it was stated that using reason to persuade refers to the use of words to persuade the audience. Most of the arguments are presented in a deductive manner. Inferences usually come in the form of formal syllogisms. Furthermore, Aristotle stated two criteria of sound arguments: (1) the argument should be valid; and (2) all the premises used in the argument are true.

A valid argument is an argument which comes up with a conclusion that follows the premises. The next criteria on premises can be a bit tricky; you should depend on your personal knowledge and skills on observation to pinpoint whether the premises are true.

Cicero's Five Canons of Rhetoric

Cicero was the one to devise the five divisions of rhetoric. Note that these canons which are based on Cicero's lessons and **Rhetorica ad Herennium** which was written by an unknown author. The canons, in a sense, are overlapping.

Cicero's First Canon of Rhetoric: Inventio/Heuresis

Inventio (Latin) or heuresis (Greek) or invention (English) refers to the art of searching for the right arguments that will best fit any rhetorical situation. In Cicero's **De Inventione**, invention was defined as the process of discovering valid or nearly valid argument to render a person's causes probable. In our modern context, invention may refer to the process of discovering strategies and using research methods to uncover useful arguments.

Cicero's Second Canon of Rhetoric: Dispositio/Taxis

Dispositio (Latin) or taxis (Greek) or arrangement (English) pertains to the text's structure or the parts of speech used. On the basis of classical rhetoric, oration was dissected into distinct parts so that it can be taught to the students during that time. Scholars who investigated on this do not always come into an argument when it comes to the parts of an oratorical speech. However, Cicero and Quintilian were able to point out six parts: (1) the introduction or exordium; (2) narrative; (3) the partition or division; (4) the confirmation; (5) the refutation; and (6) the conclusion or peroration.

Cicero's Third Canon of Rhetoric: Elecutio/Lexis

Elocutio (Latin) or lexis (Greek) or style (English) is the manner by which something is executed in terms of speech, writing, or performance. When interpreted in a narrow sense, the style pertains to the use of words, the structure of sentences, and again, the figures of speech. However, style is something that cannot be taught outright. It is a personal manifestation of the speaker. Quintilian was able to identify three style levels: (1) plain style which is used for giving instruction to the audience; (2) middle style which is used to move the audience; and (3) high style which is used to please the audience.

Cicero's Fourth Canon of Rhetoric: Memoria/Mneme

Memoria (Latin) or mneme (Greek) or memory (English) refers to the major devices and methods that can be utilized to improve the speaker's memory. According to rhetoricians from Rome, there are two kinds of memory: (1) the natural memory or the innate capability of the person to remember; and (2) the artificial memory which pertains to the method by which the natural memory can be improved or enhanced.

Cicero's Fifth Canon of Rhetoric: Pronuntiato or Actio/Hypocrisis

Pronunctiato or actio (Latin) or hypocrisis (Greek) or delivery (English) pertains to the mastering a person's gestures and voice in any discourse in any context. According to **De Oratore** written by Cicero, delivery is the highest canon in the field of oration. If not done properly, any speaker who has the strongest argument will not be able to succeed in persuading his audience. However, if a person has limited cognitive skills, but has great delivery capacity, then he is more likely to reap success in the field of public speaking.

Chapter 6: Are You A Born Speaker?

No! I remember that day I was attending a conference and the speaker was speaking extremely good, and the person who was sitting just beside me said: "wow he's a good speaker, I think he's a born speaker".

So many times we have heard this, whenever we see a

good speaker on the stage we say "wow! he or she is a born speaker". Well as a very good friend mine says "only babies are born in this world" we have to learn to speak on the stage. The way we learn singing, the way we learn dancing, we have to learn public speaking.

Speaking in front of people is a learnable skill. Like in singing we learn sa-re-ga-ma or notes and in dancing, we learn steps. In speaking we have to learn some techniques which are documented and globally used by leaders whenever they speak on the stage.

But is it so important to learn public speaking? Yes, if you wish to become a leader in your life. Because as a leader you have to separate yourself from the crowd stand alone and Speak in front of the public.

Don't try to connect with the audience

Yes, So many times we have heard this, "whenever you are on the stage try to connect with the audience. Connection with the audience is the key to public speaking"

At the same time, we have seen that people come on the stage and they fail to connect with the audience. Why? because they are not connected with themselves.

What do I mean by that? have you seen someone putting hands in the pocket or playing with the coins in the pocket while speaking on the stage? When I asked "have you told your hands to do all this" they say,"no"! It means their hands are not connected with them.

Have you seen people walking on the stage continuously from one end to another end or moving their legs in the rhythmic movement? When I asked them- "have you told your legs to walk or go back and forth?" They say "No". It means their legs are not connected with them.

Have you seen people looking here and there or up and down while speaking on the stage while the audience is sitting in front of them? when I ask them have you told your eyes to look up and down? They say "NO". It means their eyes are not connected.

Have you seen people going out of breath or breathing very fast on the stage? Their lungs are not connected. Have you seen someone speaking too fast on the stage- their tongue is not connected.

Audience connection is secondary. You will connect with the audience only when you are connected with yourself.

So next time when you are speaking on the stage make sure you ask someone to observe or make videos. And then observe it whether your hands, legs, eyes, your speed of speaking, your breath is connected or not connected. Because if all these are connected it means you are connected with yourself and then

you will be connected with the audience automatically.

Chapter 7: Visualise A Better You

You are standing in the midst of a verdant field and you can smell the freshness of the green grass around you. You are surrounded by beautiful sunflowers that are gently swaying in the breeze. The sun warmly shines over your body, giving you warm feelings all over. You feel calm and happy because of the cheerful songs of the birds and the white fluffy clouds in the sky.

If you imagined the scene I have just described, you have just experienced actual visualisation. Before you allow your doubts to settle and think that imagining a sunny day in a flower field will not help you deal with your panic, hear what I have to say first. I understand how you may not want to hear about towers in fields right now. But you need to recognise how powerful visualisation can be in dealing with your panic. You need to realise that the secret to dealing with your panic lies in the power of your mind. The human mind is a very complicated matter. Do you know that your mind is not capable of telling the difference between imagined and real situations? When you always think of negative thoughts and imagine the worst case scenarios, your mind will believe that all those thoughts are real and will push you to act according to those negative scenarios.

How can visualisation help you?

Visualisation, especially guided imagery, is very effective not only in distracting you from the negative thoughts that fill your mind but also in slowing down your heart rate and alleviating the worry that constantly hovers within your head. Research studies have also shown that it is effective in boosting your immune system. Because of those research studies, a lot of alternative mental heal experts have tried using visualisation in treating cancer patients. Even though the research studies are exploratory and uncontrolled, the results show that guided imagery can indeed increase the survival rates of cancer patients.

In panic, visualisation has been found effective in lowering the levels of fear and anxiety of patients. This means that you can become less stressed out by the day-to-day stimuli that you encounter because your mood will be enhanced and you will no longer feel hopeless. You will realise that your thoughts are different from who you really are. Even when you have negative thoughts and emotions, it doesn't mean that you are a bad person. More importantly, visualisation and relaxing for a couple of moments with your eyes closed is a great way for you to detach yourself from the demanding situation that you are in and prepare you to face your problems with a calmer and more positive outlook.

A lot of athletes all over the world are known to use visualisation in excelling in their chosen fields. A runner visualises himself at the starting line, ready to run at the go signal. He then continues to visualise how he will race around the track ahead of the other runners. He imagines the strength and endurance that he has in covering the distance. Finally, he visualises himself crossing the finish line ahead of everyone else. He imagines how the triumph and happiness he will feel. He imagines the crowd cheering him on and slapping his back for winning the race. He imagines running towards his wife and lifting her up with great joy and excitement. The more intense his imagination and emotions are, the greater the actual results are.

Visualisation can become more effective with positive thinking in easing the symptoms of your panic. It is quite impossible for your mind to dwell on negative thoughts if it is filled with happy and positive thoughts. To keep you on a positive mood, it is helpful to constantly utter positive affirmations like "I am fearless", "I am a confident talker" and "I am happy and relaxed".

When you are faced with a difficult situation, you can use positive thoughts to help you overcome the situation. You can remind yourself that you have the abilities to conquer whatever setbacks life may throw your way. Then you can use visualisation to see yourself doing the necessary steps to improve your situation. Be the star in your own movie and know that you deserve to have happy endings. When you feel like criticising yourself, bring out the list of your achievements and strengths to inspire you. Keep in mind that all those successful and happy people go through difficult times, as well. But the difference lies in their belief in themselves and how they visualise a great life for themselves.

What is Guided Imagery for panic?

With guided imagery, you utilise visualisation, words and music to around positive images that are beneficial to you. It is a misconception to think that guided imagery is only about imagining the things or situations you want to have. It is basically a process that uses the link between your mind and body that is able to generate positive transformations in yourself. A lot of mental health experts have used guided imagery in treating their patients suffering from a fear of public speaking.

Guided imagery can be likened to meditation because both involve invoking a peaceful and calm state of mind. But one of the differences between meditation and guided imagery is that in guided imagery, your thoughts are normally driven by a set of questions that guide you to create a particular image.

The objective of guided imagery is to utilise your mind in creating the effects in your body that you desire like release of releasing negative thoughts and emotions, energising and calming. During guided imagery, the right side of your brain is employed to access your spatial abilities and creativity. In this exercise, the critical side of your mind is allowed to relax so you can explore the emotional side of your brain.

Guided imagery has been proven to be effective in helping with panic by aggressively fighting negative emotions and thoughts and changing them into positive images. For instance, we know one of the most common symptoms of panic is a raised heart rate, so when you do guided imagery, you can imagine yourself sat high in a mountain top, feeling as calm inside as the Dalai Lama, and within seconds your heart rate will start to come down. If you have memories of past experiences of panic and you keep accessing them on a regular basis, you can replace those negative thoughts with images in the future where you are speaking in public with confidence, with a calm tone of voice and after see yourself being congratulated for an excellent jobs well done.

Advantages of Guided Imagery

Guided imagery can allow you to take the initiative in dealing with your negative thoughts and emotions. It is also very useful in releasing possible symptoms of panic like anxiety, stress and fatigue. Because guided imagery can be done in short sessions, you can easily integrate them into your busy schedule. Anytime you are feeling stressed out because your day to day tasks, you can instantly use guided imagery in handling the stressful thoughts before they becomes a bigger problem.

Disadvantages of Guided Imagery

If you have chronic, severe panic attacks, you also would need to consult your doctor therapist because you may need other treatments such as psychotherapy and medications.

You also need to note that there are no clinical researches that can fully support the effectiveness of guided imagery in treating panic. Although there are a lot of anecdotal evidence from various patients who have utilised guided imagery in addition to other traditional treatments.

You should also need to keep in mind that guided imagery can invoke certain difficult images so you have to be very careful when you are doing it. It is ideal that you do it with a trusted friend or loved one who can give you support in case the activity does not turn out well.

Can you do guided imagery on your own?

The answer is yes. You just need to stop and open your eyes when you need to go to the next item. But for many people, it is easier to do guided imagery with a family or friend. Your partner can read the questions while you articulate the images that you visualise. You and your partner can then discuss your answer to each question. Just make sure that your eyes are kept close during the entire session. But the best alternative to guided imagery is to do it with a therapist who has the expertise.

Guided Imagery Process

The first step in the visualisation process aims to help you determine the events or situations that trigger your panic. The next step is to help you improve your self-esteem so you will feel empowered and inspired to face and overcome whatever setbacks or obstacles lead you to panic. As you start to come up with various alternatives to improve your situation, you will start to become hopeful and see a brighter future for yourself. You will no longer feel trapped in the darkness of helplessness and hopelessness. Instead, you will be filled with light and positive emotions such as hope, appreciation and enthusiasm.

Here are the detailed steps you can follow:

Find a comfortable and quiet place where you can spend some moments to be alone without any distractions. Close your eyes. If you are doing the guided imagery on your own, read the questions at a time and close your eyes again when you are ready to perform the actual act of visualisation. When you have a partner, let your partner read the question while you keep your eyes closed.

• Determine the situation you want to change:

• Visualise the details: "Now imagine what you are currently doing. What are your reactions to the situation? Is that how you really want to react? What thoughts and emotions are you going through now?"

• Check relative sizes: "Do you see the picture as bigger that you are? If it is bigger, is it a lot bigger or only by a little?" You need to realise that if you cannot see any difference between the sizes, you may not really be dealing with the panic or perhaps you have not correctly determined the situation. You need to go back to the first questions and see if there are other situations that are more suitable.

• Change the sizes and increase your own sense of power: "Imagine yourself quickly getting bigger and taller. You can imagine how Alice in Wonderland became very tall. Take deep breaths. As you inhale, imagine yourself getting bigger."

• Broaden your horizon: "Now that you are a lot bigger, how do you see the world around you? What do you notice now that you stand taller than the person or thing that panics you? What can you see in your surrounding that you did not see when you were a lot smaller?"

• Look for new alternatives and solutions: "Now that you are bigger and you see the world from a better place, can you see any new alternatives you can take to improve your situation? What are the things that you can do now that you are bigger?"

After you have answered all of the questions above, open your eyes and think about what you have learned. If you are doing this with a partner, discuss the answers with your partner so he or she can help you analyse them. Observe how lighter and stronger you now feel. Relish the feeling of being empowered against the things that worry and panic you. Notice how you are now more inclined to think of positive thoughts instead of allowing negative thoughts to lurk inside your head. Notice how you no longer feel helpless and hopeless. Instead, you have the motivation and enthusiasm to act and improve your situation.

Chapter 8: Ways Public Speaking Can Improve Your Life

Learning to speak in public about who you are, what you do, where you come from and what you can do without fear can go a long way in expanding your social circles, building strong relations with successful people, getting yourself your dream job and representing and giving a voice to the voiceless in your community.

In this Chapter, I want to share with you some of the biggest ways public speaking can drastically improve your life

Career advancement

Effective public speaking skills can help with career advancement, as they indicate creativity, critical thinking skills, leadership abilities, poise, and professionalism, qualities which are very valuable for the job market.

Public speaking can also help you stand out at work. You'll learn to speak up in meetings, to promote your ideas, and to present yourself as a professional. Speaking skills can also help you excel in job interviews.

Helps Identify Yourself

In a very real sense, we are the sum of our communication experiences with other people. As you put together speeches on topics that you care about, you will explore your own interests and values, expand your knowledge base, and develop your skills of creative expression. In short, you will be seeking your own voice as a unique individual, a voice distinct from all other voices.

Speaking will help you develop Critical Thinking Skills

Public speaking is also a great way to build critical thinking skills. Writing a speech requires a great deal of careful thought, from the audience analysis to the outline and conclusion. It's not enough to have a message – you also need to figure out how to tailor the message to fit the needs of your audience. How can you make your points relevant to your listeners? How can you help the audience understand your views? Thinking in this way is a great exercise for improving general communication skills. If you start thinking critically about your speaking style, you may find ways to improve your general communication style at home and at work.

Speaking in Public will boost your confidence

Public speaking can significantly boost your confidence. Overcoming the fears and insecurities that accompany public speaking is empowering. Furthermore, connecting with audiences can be a strong reminder that you have valuable insights and opinions to share with the world.

Your confidence levels will grow as you go from speaking to small groups of people up to large audiences. This will benefit you not just on stage, but in everyday life as well, whether it be in a meeting or on a date.

Personal Development

Communication skills are crucial for personal and professional success. Preparing a speech forces speakers to take a step back and think critically about effective ways to communicate. In day-to-day life, it is easy to fall back on communication habits we formed many years ago. If communication is the backbone of the important relationships in your life, isn't it worth taking some time to work on? Improving your communication skills can make life more fulfilling on many levels.

Speaking in Public will help you Develop Transferable Skills

Transferable skills, such as finding information and organizing ideas, can be carried over from one context or occasion to another. So, for example, when you learn to manage anxiety in your public speaking class, you'll be able to apply that skill in other settings such as a job interview. The skills you learn in your public speaking class will help you in other communication situations as well.

Increased your social networks considerably

Putting yourself forward as a speaker makes it easier for you to meet others. You'll find people want to talk to you. You will draw people to you.

Are you looking for new ways to network and make social connections? Try public speaking. Giving a speech is like starting a conversation with a room full of people – and you can continue that conversation as soon as you step down from the podium. You and your audience share an interest in the topic of your speech, so you already have something to talk about! If the schedule allows, try to mingle with the audience after your speech, answering questions and seeking fresh perspectives on your topic. Give the audience or members the option of getting in touch with you at a later date by listing contact information on handouts or slides.

If you have a website, you can direct the audience or members to find more information there.

Speaking in Public will Increase Your Opportunities:

Your increased visibility will no doubt lead to new opportunities. In the workplace, you'll be given more opportunities to present at important meetings. Coworkers that are either afraid to speak to groups or feel they lack the charisma that you possess, will ask you to help with them with their presentations (or even request you help give the presentation). This can give you a mentoring relationship with someone at or slightly above your level in the workplace, which can be used to argue your case when it's time for promotions. It can also help you establish relationships with people outside your regular workgroup.

Expand your professional network

Another benefit of public speaking is that when you speak at an event, you will suddenly find that everyone wants to talk with you. This is a valuable opportunity for making friends, building business contacts and generating business.

Not only this, but you also get the opportunity to network with other speakers, some of whom may be very difficult to contract normally. Speaking events may also have guest rooms for speakers where they are given food and drink and can network together.

Chapter 9: The Power Of Your Words

The public speaker wants to acquire a dynamic and true collaboration with his or her audience. Therefore the choice of words is very crucial. I have compiled an interesting list of words and expressions you may want to use when you want to convey a certain message related to. Action: For examples. work, labour, realisation, build, edification, foundation, movement, throwing, push, I pull, hook, seize, promote, training, prolong, transformation, formation, reform, decision, refuse, accept, vibration. Other words can reinforce that dynamic impression such as without further ado, speedily, fast, immediately, right now, vigorous. Power: here you express yourself by speaking at the first person using verbs that evoke, without any aggressiveness, your power of decision and organisation. "I have the possibility to", "my duty is to", "I have the responsibility to", "my mission is to", "It is within my competence to", "I will personally look into", "I will instruct".

Underlining your functions

Reiterate your role, responsibilities and competencies using precise words. " in my quality as delegate", "since I am mandated by ", "I am the director, therefore", "I'm the CEO of the company and I" In essence your sentences must be constructed in such a way that they add value to the subject (I), which is the person speaking; his or her talents, power, importance without having to exaggerate but being relevant, stimulating imagination by carefully choosing your compliments and making use, if necessary, of some statistics. "The administrative division I have been in charge of for the past 15 years", "The 120 industrial enterprises of the region of which I am the main stakeholder", "The 2000 staff members I have the privilege to cater for", I am so proud to be part of the most important and most preeminent chain of companies in this region".

As a public speaker, your character and personality will often be judged by the quality and choice of words you use and how you use them. The following example list will help you utilise words that are recommended for different aspects of life scenarios.

Love: You need to show to your interlocutor or audience that you really care about them... "I am so in love with your great personality", "I love you", "I'm seduced by your charming uniqueness", "I have a lot of admiration for you", "I have, for a while, noticed your beautiful character", "I really do appreciate you"

Firmness: these are words that express a certain command, a decision or a wish. "I instruct you", "I allow you", "I will not allow", "I estimate", "I believe", "certain", "I do not permit". Some other words that show firmness include expressions and terms such as. "My decision is final", "definite", irrevocable", "the way to go", "the method to follow, "the process in place".

Fitting in your audience shoes: Here you reassure your audience that you understand and share their concerns. "I agree with you that ", "I share the same sentiment", "I too have the impression that", "I share the same opinion and this is it", "I sympathise ", I understand", "you and I share the same objectives". This is the best way to engage an audience which concerns you understand. However wish you have any objection to mention, first tell and show your audience that you fully agree with them and you understand them very well. In that case, they will, surely, be well prepared and glad to hear you out.

Calmness: imagine you have to address a very angry and dissatisfied audience! Well, my suggestion is. Before you are asked to speak, tell your colleagues you need to use the bathroom, check if the back door is still open otherwise the bathroom window will do, squeeze yourself out of that exist and run for your life without looking back! Oh! hold on! Please! Please! don't do it! Go ahead and face the music! Remember all the techniques that you have learned so far, be in charge of your audience. Your choice of words would be very crucial in this particular instance, your personality, charm and charisma will equally have a big role to play. But let us underline some of the expressions that you will find useful to engage such an audience. You will start by fitting in your audience shoes as mentioned above.Then you ask a question that will send a message of calmness and will cause your audience to see things more objectively. "Don't you think that?", "wouldn't it be more beneficial to all to calmly do it this or that way?", "Don't you think this way is too exaggerated?". Then you could add, "let us not compromise an old collaboration that's still relevant and fruitful for an ephemeral mood swing", "unrealistic demands". As you engage with such an audience it is very important that you keep a very professional calm composure at all time while trying by all means to bring calmness. That way you are more likely to impress your audience and ultimately earn their respect and trust.

How to express joy to your audience

Making a conscious effort to be joyful every day has tremendous benefits not only for a public speaker but also for the humankind as a whole. It would be a drastic mistake to carry your frustration from your house or office to an auditorium where people are so expectant to receive useful pieces of information and enjoy a great experience. so always gear up with a " piece of extra joy" in your pocket on your way to your public meeting.

Showing gratitude to your audience is one of the many ways of expressing one's joy. "I am so grateful for your ", "I thank you immensely for ", "without you this would never be possible", "I would like to express my sincere gratefulness for the job well done", "what an excellent initiative!" "Thanks to you we found the solution", "we thank God for you"

Charm: Have you ever wondered how your so admired favourite public speaker just through his or her way of saying things is able to bring his or her audience into a state of an absolute euphoria, almost like under some divine influence? And you have always wished to be like him or her right? Well, this is no magic, only one rule matters. You just need to call out the **human psychism**. Awaken the dormant child in every adult. How? Through your words and illustrations. For examples ,"I'm going to tell you a story", "once upon a time", "An old song said", " An old proverb tells us" "people living in that part of the world say ", "A great poet in the history of humanity has once said". In short, using words and expressions and illustrations that stimulate imagination and a vigorous appetite to know more.

Be sensitive: This is one the great attributes of a great public speaker. Here again, there is no magic to fit the shoe. Choosing your words carefully and the way you say or released them will make you a champion. Here are some of the useful expressions that would exude how sensitive you are toward your audience. "Believe me , I am very preoccupied concerning your grievances" , "It is not every day that I hear such touching words", "I am truly dismayed to learn that", " The infinite sadness I felt when I heard the news", "I am being embraced by the most grandiose emotion that would not let me express myself", "The pain leaves me without a voice and without recourse", "The words that have heard have profoundly touched me", "It is simply beautiful", "This is fine esthetics", "it is not a favourable atmosphere", "I feel your heart"

How to criticize without offending

Maybe you are wondering, is that even possible? Emphatically yes!in the next few lines you are going to learn one of the skills that can distinguish your from the rest and will earn you tremendous respect, especially when you have to deal with a group of employees on a regular basis.

It is possible to criticize someone without offending him or her, simply by striking the balance between the person's susceptibility and his or her self-esteem. Here two main principles that can help you achieve that. **Before you criticize**,

compliment. This means that before you say something unpleasant but necessary, you need to balance that against something more appealing or pleasant. For example," you are truly best employees and I always admire you, for your promptness and timekeeping, but please try not to come late next time". Based on this example, you interlocutor or audience would be glad to accept that you have mentioned their error because you have genuinely acknowledged their qualities. Another way of criticizing without offending is to try to relate to the person's mistake and bringing to his or her attention how you have successfully corrected the mistake. For example " Sir, a while ago, I was given the same task, and I had adopted exactly the same procedure as you did, then I spotted my mistake and resolved to rather do it this way…"

Sell yourself before others buy you

The way you present yourself to the public, your general appearance can send a message and the message could be negative or positive. But as a public speaker, you cannot afford to present yourself in a way that your audience laughs at you, whether you are aware of it or not. You will definitely make a name for yourself because people will remember you as an orator with the worse outfit ever seen. Always look your best, look presentable. It does not have to be the most expensive suit or dress in town. Even if it is the only one shirt you have, please make sure it is clean and ironed. Your outlook is just as important when it comes to public speaking because that is the first thing your audience notices.

Before you go out there and deliver your best speech ever, you 've got to feel good; and one of the easy ways to do that is to look good. Because when you look good, you feel good! And that is why your appearance is just as important and can subconsciously boost your morale and confidence.Therefore it is very important, as a public orator, to always look presentable; especially if you are to meet an audience. Remember just like in the marketing industry, you've got to sell yourself first before even people will consider listening to you and ultimately buy whatever you have to offer! Your great look of that day combined with what you will have to say will strike a very good impression, and leave something people will remember for a very long time, and that is how memory works. So remember as a public speaker it pays to look good because when you look good, you feel good indeed!

Chapter 10: Dealing With Manageable Speaking Anxieties

Remember that when we avoid the "unpleasant" experience of giving a talk then we are basically depriving and robbing ourselves of the opportunity to remedy the situation. Isn't it interesting (and quite ironic actually) that the thing that people fear most in this situation is the very thing that would cure them in the end.

Those who tend to avoid confronting their fear of public speaking deprive themselves of the opportunity to actually see how "scary" such an incident really is. With each opportunity to convey a message to the crowd you will see that the task is not so intimidating nor dangerous at all.

That means that your perceived fear is nothing more than a figment you have in your mind. Each talk you give allows you to escape from your critics intact and surprisingly whole. And each time you try you will realize that you have won a good part of the audience to your cause.

Practice Cycle to Build Up Confidence

Step 1 – Perform at Your Best: You can call the process described above as a three step cycle to building up one's confidence in public speaking. It's a cycle that I observed in myself when I was given a chance to speak in front of a local congregation once a month every Sunday. The first step is to simply give a speech and perform at your very best.

Now, my first Sunday messages were, I should say, ill-equipped. I stammered at some point. Forgot the Bible verse that I should have included. But the people loved the gospel-related story in the message and they basically identified with it.

Notice that it wasn't THE perfect talk. BUT – the congregation loved it! But the speaker hated it on the basis that there were a few bumps that needed to be worked out. The main lesson for the speaker here was that there is really no such thing as a perfect speech. Oh, let me correct the jargon part of that phrase there — there is no such thing as a "flawless speech."

You see, those who worry about making the perfect speech should redefine what they mean by the word "perfect." Nowadays when we use the word "perfect" we basically use it to mean "flawless" or "without fault." But if you look at the Greek from which that word came from you'll find a different word that will match it today. In the Greek it is rendered as teleios (τέλειος) you can look it up under Strong's Greek 5046. It actually means "full grown" or "mature." It also implies something that we should expect in the future or from a distance.

Note that you may never be able to give the perfect talk (meaning flawless) in your lifetime but you can always give the perfect talk (meaning mature and fully grown) and inspire others in spite of flaws in your delivery. It's not always about perfect delivery when you give a speech, sometimes it's all about being able to make that connection with your audience that matters.

Step 2 – Provide What the Audience Needs: The next step involves providing what the audience needs. If they came to listen to you talk about gaining spiritual healing then give them that. If they came to your presentation to hear you talk about a wonderful marketing plan that can earn them a little extra non-directional income on the side then give them that. The main thing to think about here is that you redirect your focus and attention from how you feel to what your audience needs.

One of the reasons why people get scared of giving speeches and presentations is that they are afraid of scrutiny from the crowd. To overcome this, one must have a slight paradigm shift. Sometimes you become egocentric when you deal with public speaking that you think that it's all about you. Well, it's time for you to realize that it's all about them.

To help you dwell on the point of serving your audience ask yourself these questions:

☐ How can our current set up help the audience get the most information from my talk?

☐ What would make this talk a hit in the view of my audience?

☐ What do these people need to hear most right at this minute?

☐ How can my message surprise them today?

Note that answering these questions can cause a dramatic change in your style and delivery. Ultimately, they will influence your level of confidence. It is interesting how changing one's view from being on the defensive against a judgmental mob to serving a needy crowd can increase one's confidence almost instantly.

Focus on being serviceable to your audience and then you will realize that they came with a need that you can fill. Satisfy that need and you will be better off than you were before. You'll be one step ahead of your fears. Look your audience in the eye and you'll see that a lot of them are intent on what you are saying and they actually understand whatever points you want to come across.

Step 3 – Increased Confidence Is Achieved: Take note that not everyone in the audience will like you. Not everyone in the crowd will agree with everything that you said. But there will be those who will appreciate the service that you have done. Stick around a bit for people like that who will thank you for the inspiration that they have just heard. More than just hearing the good and bad comments from the audience about your message, you will learn that experience is a great teacher – and experience builds confidence.

You will ultimately learn with experience how to deal with both positive and negative feedback. You will then be much more prepared when the next speaking engagement comes around. And from there the cycle continues.

Remember how the cycle works:

You use great delivery skills

Then you have a satisfied audience

You gain confidence from the experience

Working With Your Fears – Preparing For Your Big Day

Mark Twain once said that ""There are two types of speakers: those that are nervous and those that are liars." We'll look into that a little deeper at this point.

Making all the necessary preparation helps to build your confidence come the day when you have to deliver your speech. Studies have shown that you can calm down 75% of public speaking nerves by making a thorough preparation. You can lower that down by another 10% by learning to use proper relaxation and breathing techniques. And you can finally bring stress levels down by another 10% by accounting for your current state of mind.

Take note that there is really no way for anyone to be 100% free of any form of speaking anxiety. Even the most experienced speakers will have a certain degree of apprehension creep up on them along the way when they deliver their talks. It's a natural human response to be anxious and excited about something. That means you are in really good company – so give yourself a pat in the back.

However, you should take a holistic approach to your preparations. You should be the master of your content and know more about the topic than what you have time to present. Of course, there are other things that you need to prepare other than just your actual message to the audience. Here are some pretty good suggestions from educators and other authorities in the field of public speaking.

Prepare Your Message

If you need to do some research on the topic, in case there are some points that you need to iron out then perform a pretty extensive research on the subject. Even if you already know enough about your given topic or subject, you should do some extra research on it. Knowing more about the topic of your message can help with the nerves that usually come with a speech.

This will also help in case someone in the audience decides to throw a question or two after your speech. Don't worry the Q&A portion usually happen in private between you and the person asking the question. It's not like you're giving a press conference.

When you do your research you might want to look into issues that are also surrounding the topic. News articles, blogs, and your good old fashion magazines will be great resources. Remember that you won't have enough time to divulge all that you have researched on the topic at hand. But knowing more than you have to will bolster that inner security. It will remind you that you are indeed a worthy speaker/presenter for the said topic.

Learn Your Message by Heart

Unless you have photographic memory then it is not advisable to memorize your message word for word. Doing that will only build up your anxiety especially when the time comes for you to speak and then you forget an entire paragraph or section of your talk. That will be a disaster and may increase the tension that you are already feeling inside.

Create an outline of your message. Lay everything out including the key points that you want to make. Don't forget to include the timing of your slides, videos, and other audiovisual materials you might want to add to your presentation. Take note that even though your presentation may not necessarily be perfect and flawless but it should at least make sense.

At this point you have to practice your speech by yourself until you have a more complete grasp of your topic. You may keep the outline in your pocket or look at it in case you get lost in your practice sessions. But remember that some speaking engagements will not allow speakers to bring printed copies of their speeches with them. If you're allowed to bring a printed copy of your speech then fine but remember that your outline will be a lot better cue to help you remember.

Practice with Friends

Practicing in front of people who support and care about you will help boost your confidence. You can ask your family to listen to the speech or at least a part of it in case some people are really busy. Remember to ask for feedback to help you improve your delivery.

Another good way to practice for the mastery of your material is to discuss the topic with other people. You don't have to follow the outline you made, but all you have to do is to discuss the topic with a friend and spill out all the stuff you have learned in your research, which may even include some of the stuff you may not have a chance to mention during your actual speech.

Make a Preliminary Visit to the Venue

Some people have suggested that you visit the venue prior to the actual date when you are to give your speech. It will eventually help you get your bearings straight. It will also give you a good idea how many people will be coming to listen to you. From here you can visualize how great your performance will be. You can also test the acoustics of the place so you can immediately tell how your voice will sound during D-day.

Sit at the area where the audience will be seated. Look at the lectern and try to imagine how visible you really are to the crowd. You'll notice that they really won't be able to tell every single detail about your face or pretty much about what you're doing there. From this angle try to visualize how you will look like and how a confident looking you should look like.

Making a preliminary visit to the venue of your speaking engagement also allows you to prepare some of the technical matters of your talk. In case you're going to be using visual and audiovisual materials and aids in your presentation, this will be a good time to test how the local equipment works. In case there are technical issues with some of the equipment then you can resolve them here and now and not during the actual day of your speech. This will help solve a lot of unforeseen issues that may come along.

Challenge the Negative Self Talk

Educators from King's College of London suggest that you should challenge the negative self-talk that may come to you while you are preparing. Notice that these negative internal dialogues occur only when you keep on worrying about the speech you are to deliver. You should continue to challenge such thoughts asking for evidence until you realize that such negative thoughts actually have no bearing on reality. There is no evidence that you will fail to deliver a good presentation. There is no evidence that no one will listen to your talk.

Practice Healthy Habits

Practicing your speech is great but remember that you don't have to burn the midnight oil just to master your speech. If you find yourself skipping meals and losing sleep in lieu of practice time then you might as well hang up your gloves. Get enough sleep and eat well. This will help you maintain your focus and help you maintain mental clarity.

Keep a Healthy and Truthful Perspective

Always remember that your future and your character is not going to be defined by the speech you're about to give in a few days. Shift your bearings back to reality my friend. How well you deliver your talk won't be your defining moment.

If there are certain lapses in your delivery then so be it. It only shows that you still need to work up a few wrinkles in the way you deliver your message. It does not say anything about who you really are and where your real strengths lie.

Learn a Relaxation and Breathing Exercises

There are a lot of relaxation and breathing exercises that you can learn on your own. Take note that there will come a moment when the anxiety builds up too much that you can no longer handle it. Nervousness can either make you stop or slow down your breathing or make you hyperventilate. Figure out which of the two is your usual reaction. Learn proper breathing techniques to help you calm your nerves in either case. In case the excitement builds up too much during the day of your speech then you have to do your breathing and relaxation exercises.

Chapter 11: Should I Videotape Myself Giving A Speech As Practice?

Yes! Videotape yourself whenever possible and then WATCH it! I HATE to watch myself on tape. But it is still a great idea. It's game film. You can see things you are doing that are distracting to your audience – like moving around too much, or not enough. You get to yourself from the perspective of the audience, and that's important.

Often your client/audience will have a way to videotape you as well. I will often ask if they have the ability to videotape my talk, especially if I am doing it for a discounted fee.

Is It OK To Step Away From The Podium and Walk Around? How Much Do You Move While Presenting? What's The Importance of Body Language?

Yes, it is more than okay to step away

from the podium if you are able. Sometimes, depending on how the room is set up, you can't come out from behind the podium. Sometimes the microphone is attached to the podium and won't come off. Sometimes the podium is a table top version and therefore you are standing on the stage with a long table coming out both sides.

But if you can get out from behind the podium, do it. It gives your audience more to look at, and keeps their attention longer. It also allows you to move around and use your body more.

As a professional speaker, I often get to tell the client what I want – and so I will ask for a microphone that comes off the podium. I will also ask for enough room on the stage to move around. Sometimes this is not possible. And because I don't want to be a diva, I work with what they have.

Should I Present Differently Virtually?

Yes. There are different skills needed to present virtually. And I don't know them. I don't present virtually. But I have done a lot of interviews virtually, and there is a big difference. There's a different energy. They don't see as much of you. And you can't see the audience.

But when it comes to the words you use – the actual "speech" – there isn't a difference. But sometimes the audience's perception is different. Often in virtual presentations, they don't expect a "speech" they expect a training session with questions and answers. More of an online class. So there is less pressure to "perform" virtually than in person.

But you still need to prepare. Winging it is still not okay.

How Can I Speak With More Passion?

First of all, believe in what you are speaking about. Really think about your topic, and why it is important to you, and why you think it should be important to them. If you aren't passionate about your subject, then they won't be either.

Once you are passionate, make sure it translates in your speech. SHOW them through your words why this is so important to you. Tell them what this means to you. Be excited and act excited. Smile and gesture and move around and, well, get excited.

Think of something else you are really really excited about – maybe something that happened in your life that was super exciting – or maybe this product you found that you think is AMAZING – or maybe the music concert you went to that had you on your feet. Channel this same excitement in your speech.

It's hard to fake passion. And it's hard to learn it. But you know it when a speaker has it, and when they don't.

How Do I Pause More In Presentations?

Timing is very important in a speech, especially for comedy speakers like me. You want to give your audience time to hear what you are saying, understand it, and then think about it. You are hearing this speech for the hundredth time (hopefully) but they are just now hearing it for the first time. Give them time to let it sink in. And if your topic is really deep, hard to understand, or filled with big words, then you need to give them even more time.

The normal place to pause is at the end of a sentence. End your sentence and then wait for a second or two or even more. If you have a really long sentence, then you may want to pause in the middle. Pause after you tell a joke, or make a really powerful point.

An easy way to make yourself pause, is to have a glass of water, and plan to drink the water when it's time to pause. Don't be uncomfortable with the silence. They need these moments of silence.

Sometimes the most powerful moments in a speech are the moments when you aren't saying a word.

How Do I Keep My Hands From Moving All Over The Place?

I don't think it's such a bad thing to have your hands moving all over the place. That's the way some of us talk, and it doesn't bother me to see a speaker use their hands to help illustrate their point. In fact, I think it's really strange when a speaker doesn't use their hands, or only uses their hands occasionally as if they have scripted that movement. Yuck. I want to feel like you are talking naturally to me. And if you naturally use your hands, then keep using them. You just don't want them to be distracting. And the only way you can know this, is to tape yourself and see. And watch other speakers. Do their hand movements bother you? Sometimes I think we overthink this. Give somebody an opinion, and they will have one.

If you find that you move your hands more than you'd like to, then give your hands something to do. That might help.

Gestures are a good thing, until they become a distraction.

The Questions You SHOULD Have Asked

So, like I said, these are the questions you are asking about writing and delivering speeches. But being a professional speaker, I know what you don't know. So I want to answer the questions you should also be asking as well.

How Can I Connect With My Audience?

Speaking is all about giving a message to a group of people. You are convincing them of something. You are teaching them. You are sharing your truth. And in order to do any of this, you must establish a connection. I can talk for weeks about connecting with your audience, but for now, in this pocket guide, I'm just going to throw out six ways.

Use Humor

Tell Stories

Be Humble

Make The Speech About Them

Be Passionate

Be Different and Authentic

Are Speeches The Same As Lectures?

No. A lecture is about teaching someone something. A speech goes beyond teaching them something, and actually makes them feel something. Speeches aren't just about the transfer of content – they are about energy, and emotion, and motivation, and the experience delivered.

Chapter 12: How To Use Appropriate Techniques When Addressing An Audience Directly Or Using A Microphone/ Loudspeaker System.

Traditionally, orators have addressed the audience using their own voices and many public speakers still prefer to do so, if they can, rather than use microphones and loudspeakers because they feel that loudspeakers are 'unnatural'.

Advantages of using your own voice.

·   You can raise or lower your voice in order to emphasise.

·   It is quite easy to judge by how much you should raise or lower your voice.

·   The audience is likely to look at you rather than be aware of loudspeakers

- Your voice is likely to be quite natural sounding and not slightly 'tinny' because of the loudspeaker.

- Your hands are free to gesture.

The disadvantages of using your own voice.

- You do have to speak in a louder than normal voice

- Your voice, however loud it is, might still not be heard in a large building or by a large audience.

- Prolonged speaking can affect the voice and be tiring.

Types of microphone

Microphones are now in common use even for relatively small audiences.

A microphone may have a lead to an amplifier and then to a loudspeaker or it may be a 'radio mike' with no visible connection to the loudspeaker.

Radio mikes are more useful but do depend on a proper 'radio' link with the amplifier.

Please note that they are active while they are switched on - including before and after you speak. There are well-known examples of speakers whose 'private' remarks have been broadcast to others.

The neatest type of radio mike is one that fits onto a lapel or in a pocket. This does not restrict your movement. In fact, you can usually speak from any part of the auditorium, you can move and join your audience and still be heard. It also leaves both hands free for gestures.

The most popular type of radio mike now used by singers, entertainers and even actors is a microphone on a headset. This is a little more obtrusive but light and usually means that the voice level is consistent.

The traditional microphone, whether 'radio' or 'cabled' is a hand held 'ice-cream cornet or cone' type of microphone, much favoured by sports commentators. It is convenient and identifies you as the person speaking. You do, however, need to keep your mouth at the same distance and angle from the microphone otherwise it will not pick up your voice or your voice will fade.

The sports' mike is one designed for commentators and is held very close to the face. It is designed to keep out the wind when commentating outdoors.

Amplification and 'loud-speaking'

The ideal solution when using a microphone is that your voice is 'amplified' and transmitted via speakers to groups of listeners. This is normally unobtrusive and means that you can speak in a normal voice to a large group of people.

Loudspeaker systems bring to mind loud unclear announcements in railway stations or supermarkets with the voice echoing around the building or site.

Using such a system requires practice and skill.

- The announcer needs to learn to ignore the sound of his or her own voice.

- The voice must be pleasant and authoritative, inspiring confidence.

- The announcer or speaker has to speak very clearly indeed.

- Speaking at a slow but not unnatural speed is essential.

Both the English and the Welsh announcements in Cardiff Central Station and the station announcements in Crewe are examples of the good use of loudspeaker systems.

Chapter 13: The Structure And Outline Of A Great Speech

A great speech always appears to be delivered with ease, captures the audience's attention, and is filled with informative points, great stories, and jokes to keep you laughing. Behind the end product of a great speech is the preparation and practice that went into it. This book will help teach you how to write and deliver a great speech. It all begins with the structure and outline of your speech.

The first and potentially most important part of your speech is the introduction. This sets the tone for the whole speech and gives the audience its first impression of you. A great opening will capture their attention and leave them wanting to hear the rest of what you have to say. We'll outline great ideas for openings in a later chapter, but keep this in mind as you begin to write your speech.

After your catchy opening, dive right into the content or body of your speech. Create an outline for what the speech will be about. What are the main 3 points that you want to communicate to your audience? Start by writing these down, and then underneath these points, list examples, quotes, and stories that can back up your argument. Whether your speech is persuasive or an informative speech will determine if you use more personal stories, or if you have to research cold, hard, facts. You will want to intersperse stories and jokes throughout your speech to keep the audience engaged and awake. If you give them too much heavy, boring information, you will have lost their interest and they will be daydreaming.

Once you have written down your 3 main points and come up with the stories and examples to back them up, you need to create a conclusion for your speech. What do you want the audience to take away with them after the speech is over? What is the last main thought you want to plant in their mind from your speech? Consider these questions as you formulate your conclusion. Part of your conclusion should be a brief review of your 3 main points, and remember to keep it brief. This is not a repeat of your speech, simply a conclusion.

Lastly, end with an interesting story or quote for them to take away. Some speakers even create their own trademark phrases or closings to thank their audience for listening, and that also share their purpose and vision. If you want to create a speaking name for yourself, consider creating a unique closing that you can use for each speech. You may have heard phrases like, "Tough times never last, but tough people do!" This phrase was adopted by a famous speaker, Robert H. Schuller, and has become widely known today. Reflect on what philosophy or motto you might want to share, and incorporate this into your speech.

Remember that a great speech takes thoughtful preparation and time. By investing the time to prepare through creating an outline, introduction, body, and conclusion of your speech, you will have completed the first step to delivering a great speech.

Chapter 14: Tips And Strategies To Make Presentations With Confidence

Being able to control your fear of speaking in front of a large crowd of people is one thing; being able to present confidently is another. Here are some tips that you should take into account when making your presentations.

Know your topic. This entails a lot of research on your chosen subject or topic. The more familiar you are with what you are going to talk about, the more confident you will be when making your presentation.

This is also important in case your audience will be asking questions and clarifications about your topic. You will not be caught in the unpalatable position of being put on the spot because you do not know the answer to their question.

This does not mean, however, that you have to know everything. Even the most seasoned speakers admit to not knowing the answer to every question. It's ok to say that you do not know the answer to a particular question.

Preparedness is always a huge part of making a very good presentation.

Encourage audience participation. Very good speakers often engage the participation of their audience by asking questions and even making them share their thoughts, ideas and experiences. This is also a good strategy to bide one's time and regroup their own ideas when they suddenly find themselves "going blank".

Rehearse. The day before you make a presentation, do a dry-run or practice your presentation. This will also give you ample time to see to it that you will not run over time or end up speaking too little for the duration that you are supposed to.

Maybe you can even record yourself delivering your speech. If there is someone you trust enough to help you out, practice your presentation with them and let them critique you. They will be able to give you pointers on how to make your presentation better.

DO NOT MEMORIZE. Rehearsing does not mean you should memorize every word of your presentation. This leaves very little room for flexibility. You may end up being thrown even more off-balance when what you have memorized is not followed.

Further, memorizing tends to have another downside: it will make you lose your "voice". It will sound so rehearsed that there is a risk of sounding like an automaton.

Know your audience. You have to know who your audience will be. This way, you will know how to interact with them better when you finally take the stage and make your presentation.

Do not ignore them, either. Sometimes, the fear would cause you to look anywhere else except your audience. This is a no-no. Ignoring them will actually make your speech suffer even more.

Establish eye contact and maintain it. So you are afraid that the facial expressions of your audience will make you even more nervous? That is normal.

The solution is simple: do not over think it. Remember that people have different ways of showing agreement or disapproval. There is also the reality that you cannot please everyone, so do not let yourself be ruled by their facial expressions, since they are subject to interpretation.

Look every inch the part of a public speaker. This means you have to pay attention to your appearance. You must look presentable and neat. Wear the appropriate attire, make sure you are well-groomed, and you are dressed exactly right for the audience you will be speaking to and the topic you will be discussing. However, make sure that your appearance does not upstage your topic.

Talk about what you know. As much as possible, you should talk about issues or subjects that you truly care about, or you feel strongly about. In instances where you have to speak in public about something you do not really care about, try to drum up some interest in it. Read on the subject, find angles that you find interesting, and work from there.

Public speaking is meant to provide value for both the speaker and the audience. It is meant to be informative, motivating and entertaining. Aim to accomplish one or several of these.

Perfection should not be your goal. Trust me, nobody is. Instead of striving to give the perfect presentation, give your best effort to providing a presentation that will get your message across. Mistakes are inevitable; it's how you fare through it that counts.

Finally, remember that we are all born without the ability to speak or utter a word. Accept that nerves are natural, and that it is absolutely acceptable to be nervous, particularly before facing an audience to speak. It is then up to the person on whether he or she will use those nerves work to his or her advantage, or let them drive him or her to run and hide. The adrenaline rush that makes you nervous? Turn it around and use it to fuel your passion towards your speech.

Speaking is something that is learned over time. Therefore, believe in yourself and believe that you can overcome your fear of speaking in front of other people – regardless of how large the crowd is – and deliver a presentation in a calm, competent, and confident manner.

Chapter 15: Talk! Don't Read

Now is the day of your big performance. You are excited and anxious to speak to your audience. It always helps to start with a few light comments and then get into your material. Recall how you want your speech look as natural as possible? This is actually one of the most crucial factors that you need to apply when it comes to public speaking. Consider your listeners as people. People tend to lose interest when it comes to topics that are too complicated. Therefore, you also need to make your topics somewhat loose and natural. Instead of being too technical while delivering your talk.

Now, you need to know the difference between free talking and reading. Free talking is based on paraphrasing and unrehearsed speaking. It involves talking about a certain topic without the use of complex terms or analogies. Reading your speech is the opposite of free talking.

When you start reading your speech, you are unable to rephrase your words and you cannot practice proper hand gestures. Your eyes are also focused more on the piece of paper that you are holding instead of the crowd. It is very important for you to learn to practice free talking rather than reading.

Free talking involves proper analysis and deeper understanding about your topic. At first, you need to read and comprehend your topic. You need to absorb every detail and every bit of information about the topic that you have prepared. Once you have soaked yourself with information then you need to learn how to present it to the crowd. Follow your mental outline and go from there. Your mental outline will be your guide in order to chronologically present your speech without hopping from one subject to the next.

However, there are some topics which are quite hard to comprehend. If you are faced with this issue, then you need to learn when to read. There are actually two ways to present your topic while reading to the crowd. One of which is through the use of visual aids and the second is through the use of a summary note. Summary notes are important since they are used to help you present complex terms and analogies. If you are going to have a challenging topic then you certainly have to use those summary notes. Summary notes are composed of small paragraphs and key terms about your subject. Never make a note which has bulk sentences and paragraphs.

Chapter 16: Learn To Coerce Nicely--Use Your Charm!

While not everyone was born with charm, it does not mean it can no longer be developed. According to the **American Psychological Association** (APA), people who know how to endure hardship, and who are willing to improve themselves can develop charisma—especially when they're willing to have a positive outlook in life.

Take note that charisma is not automatically linked with physical beauty—and that's why you can do so much about it. It's not about changing your whole personality, but rather about trying to improve yourself so you can have the X-factor—that will make doors of opportunities open up for you.

Read on and find out how you can help yourself develop some charisma.

Presence—and Body Language

First up is developing presence, and knowing proper body language. These are deemed to be important aspects of one's personality. Even without saying a word, having the right body language can help you exude likability and warmth.

Presence, meanwhile, is all about you making sure that you are attentive enough. In a classroom for example, you might notice that there are people who go to class, and who are physically present—but are mentally absent. And guess what? No one wants to be around those kinds of people for the sole reason that it's like being with a robot. And even if the world today has all these modern items, it's still best to be with people who have hearts—and who know how to give attention not only to themselves, but also to others.

Learn to Feel Good About Yourself, as Well

You also have to realize that a charming person is someone who allows others to feel good about themselves, too. If you've ever seen **The Hills**, you'll realize that

Whitney Port, although she was not the most popular of the bunch, she still knew how to get people's attention because she thrived on giving compliments. By making others feel good about themselves, they saw her as a friend, rather than an enemy—and it really worked for her benefit.

You can do the same, too. Instead of being arrogant and always making people feel like they're second best, why not make people feel like they can actually do amazing things, too? You see, when you help people feel good about themselves, you make them see you as someone they can trust, and you get to create an environment of positive energy—and these days, that is totally important.

Here are some exercises that you can try in order to develop proper body language, charm, and presence:

Practice the right body language. For starters, this means standing up straight, making sure your head and your back are up, and making open movements. This will make people realize you're willing to talk to them, and that you are not holding back.

Be animated. When talking to people, try to make it seem as if you are telling them a story, and that you are not lecturing them. Smile with your eyes! Be natural.

Smile, especially while giving compliments. This would make the said compliments real, instead of just making it seem like you're just going through the motions.

Give people sincere praise—and be humble about your achievements. For example, if a person was praised at work today, go ahead and give her more praise—but don't go saying that you can do what she can, too.

Don't be selfish. When asked for help, go ahead and help others out. It will make you feel better about yourself, too.

Avoid the following mannerisms: touching your face, shifting your weight from side to side, playing with your fingers, touching your ears, putting hands in your pockets, fixing your clothes over and over again, crossing the arms, pacing back and forth, **and** adjusting your hair.

Practice active listening. This means that you will listen not only to the words people say, but to what those words mean. You learn to read between the lines, and understand that listening to people means you listen to understand, obtain information, learn, and enjoy—all at the same time. Here's how you can do it:

a. Pay attention. Look at whoever's talking directly.

b. Show that you're listening.

c. Be ready to provide feedback, and to defer judgment for later.

d. And, make sure to respond appropriately. Do not be biased.

You see, by being in tune with your emotions, you also learn to understand what others are going through. You do not become prejudiced or judgmental. Instead, you learn how to see where they're coming from—and you begin to realize that people really have different lives to live. Then, they begin to relate to you, and know that you're someone they can trust—and that's exactly what you want to happen.

Chapter 17: What To Avoid When Speaking In Public.

There are some things which are common characteristics of inexperience. Foremost among these is showing hesitancy; 'umm' , 'err', 'like', and similar fillers. Any schoolteacher will tell you that these are common amongst children when asked to deliver a short speech as part of their English curriculum. Silence is better but it takes a degree of self-confidence to be able to stand without saying anything. This needs to be practiced.

Other common misapprehensions about what is acceptable follow:

· Emphasising yourself rather than the job in hand: " Unaccustomed as I am to public speaking".

· Stating, "I'm sorry if I sound nervous" and thus confirming everybody's perception that you are nervous. This might be 'cute' and acceptable in a family occasion such as a wedding or naming ceremony where people know you. It is not advisable in formal public speaking

· Casting doubt upon your competence to speak about the topic. Statements such as: "I haven't really given this much thought"; "I don't really know much about this"; "I'm surprised I've been invited to talk to you about this"; "You need someone more qualified/experienced to talk about this".

· Apologising in such a way that it casts doubt on your credibility, your ability to explain or the quality of your preparation. "I'm sorry, I didn't explain that very well, I'll try again"; an explanation followed by, " I suppose"; "I'm sorry, that diagram is very messy"; "That photo is out of focus". The audience will forgive your poor photograph if you explain that you were being chased by a lion at the time, otherwise they'll conclude that you didn't try hard enough to produce a proper photograph or couldn't be bothered to prepare properly for your speech. This shows disrespect to your audience.

- Poor timing. "I've been speaking too long and will have to rush the next bit". "I don't have time for conclusion I've prepared- so I'll just say…"

- Using language incorrectly e.g. malapropisms.

"The police are not here to create disorder, they're here to preserve disorder." - Richard Daley, former mayor of Chicago More examples can be found at

http://examples.yourdictionary.com/examplesofmalapropism.html#ZIqAOvZCuKuuBXGh.99

- Using words that have a different cultural value from what you thought e.g. 'tatsächlich' in German does mean 'indeed' or 'to be correct' but is very much stronger. It is equivalent to stating. "You are wrong and I am now going to correct a factual error you have made."

Lack of experience

Where there is lack of experience, speakers do not meet common expectations such as:

· A lack of an effective start -because there is no attention grabbing beginning - No story or anecdote, for example, but a statement such as "I'm going to talk about X, then Y , then Z, then I'll finish with A. It is, however, a good idea to indicate briefly what you are going to say – while the audience's attention is still fresh. Going into too great a detail is not helpful.

· Having no ending. "Well I've finished saying what I wanted to say"; "That's all folks". The latter might well suit the end of a series of cartoons, but it does not end a speech properly.

· Making the structure of your speech too obvious, "firstly, secondly, fifthly"

Other common faults when speaking

· Garbling your speech, so that listeners cannot understand. Your diction must be clear.

- Express train delivery – usually of a speech that has been learnt off by heart or reading all of a speech quickly "to get it over with" from a script.

- Reading aloud with an artificial intonation every word of a script that has obviously been written as an article or literary essay.

- Not projecting your voice at all (even with a microphone) so that it seems to stop before reaching the audience. This fault is made worse by looking down at the script and not looking at the audience and engaging with them.

- Grimly holding on to or hiding behind a lectern so that there are no natural gestures and no movement from the spot.

- Not looking at the audience at all (because you are reading a script).

- Not respecting the courtesies by not addressing the chair, audience, and by not saying thanks.

- Drawing attention to yourself rather than your speech because of some nervous ticks such as tapping the lectern, keeping your hand(s) in your pocket, jerky head or hand movements, shuffling your feet, or moving up and down like a jack in the box.

The above are quite long lists of 'not to do" things but they are the converse of the good practice encouraged elsewhere in this book. If you feel that you exhibit some of these characteristics then a 'critical friend', a tutor or a therapist/medical practitioner might be able to help you.

A few years ago, I was teaching an Entrepreneurship course to a group of adult learners and for a final assignment, I split the class members into groups of five and then asked each group to research a medium-sized American company using criteria that I assigned. Their final grades were going to be based on their research and PowerPoint presentations that their groups would present to me, their class members, and a few invited guests.

All five groups did a credible job of researching their chosen company making their oral presentations, but a few of the PowerPoint presentations had issues that took away from their lectures. The biggest lesson I learned as an instructor that day was that I needed to put more time into teaching the basics of PowerPoint presentations if I was going to require them for grades. **Here are some solid tips regarding slide presentations you should consider as you prepare them:**

Limit the Amount of Text You Include on Your Slides. If your slides contain too much text, audience members don't know whether to listen to what you are saying, to read the text on your slides, or to try and do both at the same time, which proves to be impossible and thus frustrating. Slides that contain too much writing distract from a speech. In addition, it is never a good idea to read directly from a slide because it is a duplication of efforts. Keep your text-oriented slides concise and precise.

Make Sure That You Proofread Your Slides. There is nothing quite as glaring as a misspelled word, or improper grammar, or a typographical error on a slide. Just yesterday, I sat in on a webinar that was very professional in every manner except the presenter spelled the word "rich" as "rick!" There it was, that typo glaring out at me, taunting me, daring me to drop the guy an email and let him know that that one typo totally threw me off his entire presentation!

Always use the spellchecking component on the software you are using to produce the slide. In addition, it is a very good idea to ask a colleague or a friend to read through your slides because a second set of eyes may pick up mistakes that your eyes and your spellcheck program were unable to notice. If you can't find anyone to proofread your slides, step away from your work for at least a half hour or so, and then go back and re-read the work.

Taking a break from your work may allow you to "reset" your ability to see mistakes you could not see before.

Avoid Using Excessive Bullet Points. Using too many bullet points will decrease the effectiveness of your main message. Save your bullets for the main ideas and concepts that you are discussing in your speech.

Choose Appropriate Color Schemes for Your Slideshow. This is my weakness. I have no sense of color and, for that reason, I always ask my assistant to choose colors for my slide presentations because she has an eye for that sort of work. Presentation software programs usually have a variety of color schemes from which you can choose. The use of colors in your slide presentations should be appropriate to the subject matter and not distract the viewer from the content of the presentation.

Limit the Number of Slides in Your Presentation. The trick when you are using slides or visuals is to create a balance. If your presentation is going to be billed as a speech, you have an obligation to make sure your oral presentation is the focus of the presentation. Use slides to emphasize key points in your speech, rather than create a slide for everything you touch upon as you orally present.

Do Not Try to Pack Too Much Data on a Slide. Slides should be as easy for your audience to understand as your speech. Keep your slides clean and make sure your graphs, pie charts, and diagrams are legible and succinct enough so that those on the receiving end of your presentation can easily read and comprehend them.

Limit Your Use of Animation as You Create Your Slides. Remember that your presentation should be geared toward sharing and developing an idea with your audience. The method you choose to share that information should enhance that communication, not distract from it. While there are certainly times when animation is appropriate, make sure that your animation adds to the message you are attempting to convey.

Take Care to Choose a Font that is Appropriate to Your Message. There are plenty of fonts included in presentation software from which to choose. Select a font that is legible from a distance and is attractive to the reader.

Another important decision presenters must figure out if they are planning on using visual media during a presentation is whether to use an assistant, or a "producer" to assist with the presentation. Producers can greatly enhance the visual presentation by operating the device that is displaying media to your audience. If you choose to ask a producer to work with you, make sure that you practice your presentation with the producer ahead of time so that you can get your timing down and work out a signaling system that will not distract the audience, if you need a signaling system.

To summarize, visual presentations can be great tools as presenters seek diverse ways to persuade and to present information to their audiences. Like any other component of a presentation, though, presenters need to put in the time, energy, and effort to design visual presentations that enhance audience members' experiences, not confuse or clutter it. If possible, run through your slide presentation with a trusted person (or persons) who is able to critique and give you honest feedback before you present in front of your audience. Never forget that the better your preparation, the better your presentation.

Questions to Ponder:

What do I need to learn in order to improve my ability to create a powerful slide presentation?

Who do I know that will give me honest and critical feedback regarding my slide presentations?

Chapter 18: You Are Not Alone

You've known that you would be speaking for just ten minutes at a meeting for the past three weeks. Plenty of time to prepare and become confident with your subject matter. Besides, it's only ten minutes. But ever since you got the assignment to speak, you've been dreading it. And every time you think about it, you get nervous. Actually, you get beyond nervous. You get nauseous, your hands get clammy, your mouth gets dry, and your heart starts to race. You become very anxious.

As a child, even raising your hand in class to answer a question filled you with dread. You knew the answer. But when you raised your hand, everybody in class turned to look at you. And that one moment could be when it started.

Remember when you were four or five-years old (probably not, but anyway) and you gladly got up in front of everybody in the living room to dance, sing a silly song, or do awkward cartwheels? It's because you had 100% encouragement! Every person watching you applauded and asked for more. It was a rarity if somebody critiqued you or made you feel anything less than perfect.

When my nieces were young, they would put on variety shows in my mother's backyard. They would set out chairs for us to be their audience, make cookies (and sell them to us) and put on little skits to entertain us. We gave them standing ovations. As they got older, we were still their best audience, but none of them wanted to be vulnerable in front of others.

When I ask people when they first noticed the fear, they say they've always had it. I remind them of the above-mentioned scenario: entertaining the family in the living room (or backyard). I tell them that I bet their parents even have pictures of these theatrics. Their body language changes and they smile. Somewhere along the way, things changed. Now, getting up in front of a group of people is one of the most terrifying things for them. They are not alone.

I have watched many people who have to deliver a presentation, and their fear is palpable. I know you've seen them, too. It's almost painful to watch. Public speaking should be the opportunity for you to influence others. We all have to do it at one time or another. If you view it as "have to," it will be an unpleasant task instead of an opportunity.

Everybody who has a fear of public speaking truly believes they're the only person who feels that way. They really believe everybody else in front of the room is completely at ease. Well, at least, most of them.

Barbra Streisand had an experience while on stage that kept her from performing publicly for three decades. One night while on stage, she forgot the lyrics to a song. She couldn't just shrug it off. She is a self-professed perfectionist. After 30 years, she went back onstage in Las Vegas. To this day, she insists on a teleprompter to help her through her performance.

Warren Buffett was so terrified of public speaking that he enrolled in a public speaking course in college and dropped out of it before it started. He once said, "If you can't communicate and talk to other people and get across your ideas, you're giving up your potential."

Joel Osteen speaks to over 40,000 people every Sunday at the Lakewood Church. When he took over the helm for his father, he was scared to death. The negative comments he heard comparing him to his dynamic father absolutely crushed the small amount of self-esteem he had. Words, he says, are like seeds. If you dwell on them long enough, they take root and you will become what those words say you'll become—if you let them. Osteen says negative labels—those people place on us and the labels we place on ourselves— prevent us from reaching our potential.

Before you can delve into the meat of this book, you need to change your paradigm of public speaking. A paradigm is simply a way of looking at something. If you are already pre-determining failure in your presentation, I assure you, you will fail. A paradigm shift is changing how you look at something. Be open-minded as you go through the chapters of the book. Take your time and commit to following the structure I created for you.

If you take this information and set a realistic expectation of the outcome, you will be successful.

What you tell yourself, is your truth. Never, ever underestimate the power of the conversations you have with yourself.

Chapter 19: Stories And Anecdotes

"Once upon a time the prince met the princess. But she was having a bad hair day, and he was interested in her brother, so they both lived somewhat happily ever after, but not with each other."

"Stories are not just meant to make us smile. Our lives depend on them."

Chinua Achebe, Nigerian novelist

Gathered around the warm fires, listening to the Wise Ones, hearing the history through the Storyteller was the way of our ancestors. It was an honor to be the Storyteller, as the Storyteller spoke the truth of the moment, sharing the wisdom and knowledge that guided the people and protected the children.

"We come back to the WORD as the starting point of all Creation."

Ernest Holmes, The Science of Mind

Our **culture** has **storytelling roots**. Everything we do well contains a story. Our movies and TV programs tell stories. we sell with a story, we relate to each with stories. Our speeches and talks follow the pathways of good stories. All the great teachers — Jesus included — were great storytellers. In this day and age all the geat speakers are great storytellers. Storytelling is an art.

"The truths of how to live in harmony were kept alive by wise Storytellers."

James Sams and Twylah Nitsch

We love stories and **we learn through the telling of them**. Sprinkle your message with stories, anecdotes (analogies and examples) that bring out the flavor of your theme. Stories, anecdotes, jokes and illustrations take the audience by the hand and help them understand what you're saying. Stories deliver the salient points of wisdom. You can tell us the point you're trying to make, and we may understand it, but **we get the meaning through stories**. We're a storytelling culture.

Jack'S TiDBIT:

1) Give me information…it's in my head

2) Tell me a story…it's in my heart

3) Involve me…it's in my gut

The stories that affect us the most are personal stories, experiences that moved us. Regardless of the kind of story, bring us into it. Great storytellers suspend our realities and make us think it's happening right now.

ABOUT STORYTELLING

- The ability **to** exchange experiences **is at the heart of** genuine storytelling

- Forever, we have relied on stories to **make sense** of our lives

- **Stories are the** building blocks of knowledge.

- **Stories are the** playground for language

- **Stories** offer a deeper understanding **of our** origins
- **Stories** teach **us** how to be human.
- Stories **help us know who we are** in new and unforeseen ways.
- **Stories** organize the things that happen to us.
- Stories offer a deeply meaningful and intimate **legacy**
- **Stories** create community
- **Stories help us to** see through the eyes of other people
- **Stories show us the** consequences of our actions
- **Stories** educate our desires
- Stories help us **dwell in place**
- **Stories** liberate us into a realm of timelessness.
- Stories help us **dwell in time**
- Stories **contradict** our extreme **isolation**

- **Stories help us** deal with suffering, loss, and death
- **Stories** acknowledge the wonder and mystery of Creation
- Checklist of Essential Story Items

All the great stories contain the following ingredients:

1. **OPENER.** Transport us to **another time and place** with your very first sentence. Or introduce us to someone, or to some meaningful experience. Example: "My mother wears a man's toupee." Or "They closed the school on my 6th birthday." "During the week, she was just a secretary."

2. **SENSES AHOY**. Use **colorful, crunchy, juicy, smelly, happy, scary, exciting words.** Words which make us see, hear, smell, taste, touch and feel. Go for economy. These descriptive words should convey a MAXIMUM AMOUNT OF THOUGHT IN A MINIMUM AMOUNT OF WORDS.

To find them we must ask the following questions:

a. What did the **people and places look like** in the story? (tall, short, fat, skinny, crooked, green, yellow, white)

b. What were the **sounds**? (ocean, wind, dogs) How did the **people talk**? (fast-talking, lisp, slow drawl)

c. What **smells**? (lilac, perfume, bakery shop)

d. What **textures**? (Hands like leather, smooth as a baby butt)

e. How did the **people feel**? (angry, afraid, confused, happy, sad)

3. **MAGIC MOMENTS**. Really great stories have Magic Moments. A magic moment happens when the **storyteller stops telling the story** from the narrator's point of view and **becomes one of** the **characters** (by using that character's voice and body movements). This is when the storyteller transforms from telling the story in 3rd person style and we are suddenly **in the**

story (1st person.) (As I said in the very beginning, being a speaker and a performer are all the same thing to me. If you want to pop to the top, see yourself as a performer — not just a speaker.)

4. **CHALLENGE IS COMING**.* Not every story has this, but it's nice when they do. This is also called the **build up**. What in the story makes you feel that **trouble is coming**? Example: "Ronald was always so careful driving to work." (We know Ronald's about to get into trouble.)

5. **CHALLENGE/ Pain.*** The **crisis** or **peak moment.** Moment of truth. Often called the "Once Moment" because the word "once" will always let you know if you have a peak moment. Example: "Once Ronald decided to try a new way to work, all hell broke loose." Trouble isn't necessarily a bad thing. Trouble just means that the world we know is turned upside-down. Trouble in a story can mean we just got a big inheritance and this is not a bad thing at all.

6. **CHALLENGE OVERCOME.*** How did the **main character get out of the troublesome situation**? What resource or intrinsic human value did our hero have to tap into? Example: "Ronald finally made it to work that day — but he didn't get much done."

7. **CLOSER.** Close your story with a **powerful sentence. This is a great place for the moral**, or for what the main character — and consequently the audience — learned from the story. Example: "Ronald knew he would never drive again — not without seat belts."

Some of this material courtesy of Karen Golden

[*: **Steps 4-6 are optional**. Some inspirational stories aren't built around crisis, but the best of them are. Conflict and resolution have been the soul centers of storytelling since we learned to communicate. Go to any movie. You can graph out the conflict and resolution, and in far too many of them, you can time it.]

The speaker's task is to make the difficult easy for the audience to understand. Stories help to do this. They can take dry facts, statements and statistics and make them infinitely more memorable to an audience.

The best speakers are all great storytellers.

Jack'S TiDBIT:

Keep a record of your stories, anecdotes, jokes and great quotes. Put them in a folder, journal, or computer file, so when you need them, they're easily accessible. Practice your stories. Tell them to a friend, try them out in different ways. Eliminate superfluous parts and irrelevant details.

Chapter 20: Brief Introduction

One of the most useful yet challenging skills one should have in any field is the public speaking & communication ability. Effective public speaking skills give the edge over others in personal, public & most importantly in professional life. Although it is one of the core skills one should possess to be a successful one, but most of them find it difficult to deliver it.

Need of public speaking

☐ Public speaking increases a person's self-confidence. It is directly related to the self-confidence that is more you do practice, more self-confidence you will get in return.

☐ Public speaking is a great way to show someone's abilities, knowledge, strategies in any topic or field. People with good public skills are always given more importance over others.

☐ Public speaking helps one to reach a large number of people in a very short time & in an effective way rather than conducting individual conversations.

☐ Good public speaking skill is one of the major requirements for any job seekers. A good public speaker is always preferred over others by any recruitment company.

☐ It helps one to go up in their career path. An employee is always expected to have good public speaking & communication skills for the purpose of business communication.

Transactional model of communication in public speaking

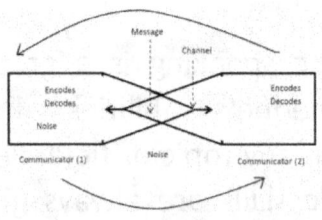

☐ Process of effective public speaking can easily be understood by the Transactional model of communication. In this model, the communication is considered as the circular process between the communicators. Communicators refer to the people who participate in the interaction during the speech that is the speaker & the audience.

☐ Encoding involves the process of changing mental images & its associated words into speech in order to convey the message. On contrary to that, decoding involves the process of turning the words into mental images.

☐ The communicators involve in encoding & decoding the verbal & nonverbal behaviours, collectively called as Message. Verbal behaviours include the words that we speak while nonverbal behaviours include voice tone, personal appearance, posture, gesture, eye contact between the communicators etc.

☐ Effective public speaking is the result of proper transactional model of communication. Hence, both the audience & the speaker must participate equally to make it alive throughout the entire speech.

☐ However, if the audience & the speaker have differences like interests, age group, point of view or any other situational differences; in that cases, transactional model will not take place & will result a poor speech & communication between the communicators. This is why, it is very much important to analyse the audience to deliver an effective speech.

Chapter 21: Qualitative Descriptions

Activity

Ramzi Abou Ghalioum

Topic: Describing the qualities of everyday phenomena and objects

Learning Objectives: This learning activity provides an opportunity for students to:

Demonstrate a conceptual understanding of associative language.

Utilize relational language and improve efficiency in their use of descriptive adjectives.

Reinforce the basic communication skills necessary to effectively deliver a speech.

Description of Activity: Pick an everyday object or phenomenon and describe one characteristic of it (color; tactile quality; smell; taste; or sound) without using adjectives pertaining to that characteristic. (for example, if someone were describing the tactile qualities of a smooth round ball, they would have to use the associated emotions they feel when coming into contact with the smooth ball and describing it that way).

Materials needed: **None**

Prep time for students: 15-30 minutes (dependent on class time)

Assignment time: 2-3 minutes per student (dependent on class time)

Instructions for Instructor: I usually begin by discussing Plato's Allegory of the Cave, which is what inspired the idea for this activity, to the students.

I then describe to them the activity and provide for them an example, such as, "let's say you wish to describe the smell of a chocolate chip cookie. Rather than attempting to describe it by utilizing other adjectives pertaining to the olfactory sense, tell me what thoughts, feelings, and senses you associate with a chocolate chip cookie. Does it remind you of your childhood? Of Christmastime? How do those memories make you feel? Did you used to dunk chocolate chip cookies in a tall glass of ice-cold milk? What sounds does a chocolate chip cookie make you hear?"

Inform the students of the time they have to write out their responses (I afford them 20-25 minutes; I find that this activity works best if they have time to think about a response before they write it out).

Instructions for Students:

Take some time and think about an object you wish to describe using the qualitative descriptors we just discussed.

Prepare a presentation, detailing that object/phenomenon and providing the listener with as many details as possible.

You will have 20-25 minutes to prepare a 2-3-minute presentation.

When it is your turn, stand up/come to the front of the class and deliver what you have written.

Necessary Background: This activity, as mentioned, was inspired by Plato's Allegory of the Cave and the difficulty one has in attempting to explain personal sensory experiences.

Although the activity is performed in front of an audience, its goal is to promote lateral thinking and concept-association.

Debrief: This activity, even for adults, is quite difficult. I often end the activity by explaining to the students the idea of "qualia" and how it is impossible to explain ideas like smell and color because they are inherently experiential in nature. This validates the difficulty they felt in attempting the activity.

Variations: I began the activity by having students only describe color, but expanded it in order to accommodate students who may be color-blind.

Trouble spots: Students might not come up with a full 2-3 minutes and might describe something very briefly. It is important to tell them that they must attempt to make this time and to encourage them to delve as deeply into their descriptions as they can.

Common questions students ask:

Can I use other senses to describe it?

Can I look it up on my phone?

I can't do it.

Chapter 22: Size Matters

Room size that is. Knowing the size of the space affects how you design and deliver your presentation.

Is it a meeting room? A wedding reception hall? A conference room? Will you need a microphone? How will the people in the back of the room hear you if there isn't a microphone?

Let me illustrate.

A large audience had been assembled for a presentation on fraud awareness and internal controls (a compulsory requirement to meet organisational accreditation). We had been expecting at least 30 on site and another 45 to 50 on 'video conferencing' (VC) from four locations (VC - could also be known as Very Clunky). I have yet to experience a VC work as it is meant to. Generally the presenter fails to engage those on the video conference end and the camera set up is such that all you can see of your remote audience is waaaay down the other end of the room showing body language which suggests they are either working on something else or they are asleep (or in fact, absent). It might start off with half a dozen in the remote location but take your eyes off them and you might turn back to find a bunch of empty chairs.

Back to the story of the large audience with remote video from four locations.

As it turned out the room booked for the local delegates could hold approximately eight delegates – 35 were waiting in the hall.

Right.

No-one seemed to know what to do.

Ok, let's move another small group which was booked into a larger meeting room and use the video conferencing available in both rooms. Just let the remote attendees know that there will be a delay.

Right oh.

Everything set up. Switch on the video conferencing. Nothing. Fiddle a few cords, re-plug some leads. Nothing. "Oh yes", says the organiser, "I forgot we had some problems yesterday – can't be fixed until next week and there's no local IT support, cost cutting you know"

Ok.

All the remote delegates are told that the class will be tomorrow using a different dial in method – goodbye.

The remaining onsite delegates stayed and completed the training crammed into one room using the projector we had bought as backup.

The following day the venue had been moved and apparently the systems were working. We set up only to find we can see them but they can't see us. The solution meant that we ran the presentation live and on video-conferencing. Worked reasonably well except the audio was out of sync on videos but we did note that at the end of the session at least two of the four external venues seemed to be deserted. Remote training must be riveting.

I hate video conferencing. Webinars can be more successful but even they are lousy if you have activities or have a highly interactive presentation style.

For those presenting training or speaking in an unknown location, **never** assume the client understands your needs to deliver a quality product.

Find out about the -

Room and table layout

Room size

IT availability (and contact person for problems)

Screen (is there one?)

Whiteboard, (whiteboard) pens and eraser

Projector – do they have one and someone who knows how to use it?

Do your IT connectors match those of the venue (HDMI vs VGA)?

Are you responsible for set up and clean up?

Are you allowed/able to change the room setup?

What is the venue access time? (What time can you arrive to set up? Is there another event in the room before yours?)

Is there venue support staff?

Lesson 11 – Be acquainted with the space you are going to present in and what equipment will be available

If you are required to present to a board, committee, conference or at your mate's wedding try to visit the venue beforehand. Regardless of the purpose of the talk you have to give, feeling comfortable in the space will help you reduce the risks of feeling outside your comfort zone.

Peer Groups Can be the Most Difficult

Audience reactions and engagement level vary widely. After years of presenting and facilitating, my greatest challenge has been where the audience might know more than me, actually does – or worse, thinks they do.

One particular group from years ago springs to mind.

The long-term unemployed cohorts who were unintentional class mates for each of the eight week course were usually an incredibly diverse range of individuals – by age, ethnicity, education, experience and personal stories. Then, as fortune would have it, one group consisted of all similar in age to me, university graduates and from 'good' backgrounds. All of them were 'accidentally' unemployed. What else they had in common was attitude. It took some time for me to figure out why I wasn't connecting with this group. Collectively I couldn't get them involved in discussions or participating in activities (except with overt reluctance). Yet individually, outside the classroom, they were keen to talk, laugh, share thoughts and ideas with me – but back in the classroom, a brick wall of recalcitrance.

I can be a bit slow on the uptake sometimes but I did eventually identify the common problem. It was me. Not the personal 'me' but the 'me' who was them but employed. Collectively they wanted to catch me out and identify that I was no better than them (and I wasn't). I also felt that as they were all around the same age and skills level it was like teaching a high school class where no-one wants to stand out by asking questions or being first.

Lesson 12 - know your audience; every group will be different, even if they are the same

Note: peers can be your harshest critics and your biggest challenge to impress – in the nicest possible way.

Conclusion

Thank you again for downloading this book!

I hope this book was able to help you to understand your fears, face them and conquer them to become a Confident Public Speaker.

The next step is to watch a couple of those video, get some inspiration and get to work on the qualities you will need to be successful in this field.

Following these tips will not happen in a day and so don't try that and get demotivated. Keep all these points in mind and start practicing them and it will gradually become a habit and you will become a great public speaker and your fears will become history.

Thank you and good luck!

www.ingramcontent.com/pod-product-compliance
Lightning Source LLC
Chambersburg PA
CBHW072014070526
44583CB00015B/1474